WE MAKE THE ROAD BY WALKING

Edited by Brenda Bell, John Gaventa, and John Peters

Myles Horton and Paulo Freire

We Make the Road by Walking

Conversations
on Education and
Social Change

 Temple University Press
Philadelphia

Temple University Press,
Philadelphia 19122
Copyright © 1990 by
Highlander Research and
Education Center
Published 1990
Printed in the United
States of America
The paper used in this
publication meets the
minimum requirements
of American National
Standard for Information
Sciences–Permanence
of Paper for Printed
Library Materials,
ANSI Z39.48-1984 ⊗
Library of Congress Cataloging
in Publication Data
Horton, Miles, 1905
We make the road by
walking : conversations
on education and social
change / Myles Horton
and Paulo Freire ; edited
by Brenda Bell, John Gaventa,
and John Peters.
p. cm. Includes
bibliographical references.
ISBN 0-87722-771-3
1. Education – Philosophy.
2. Social change.
3. Freire, Paulo, 1921. –
Views on social action.
4. Horton, Myles, 1905. –
Views on social action.
5. Adult education – Social
aspects – United States.
6. Education – Social
aspects – Brazil.
7. Highlander Folk School
(Monteagle, Tenn.)
I. Bell, Brenda. II. Gaventa,
John, 1949.
III. Peters, John Marshall,
1941. IV. Title.
LB885.H64W4 1990
374–dc20 90-36005

Contents

Preface

Myles Horton and Paulo Freire knew about each other more than twenty years ago. Paulo read part of the growing literature about Myles and Highlander, and Myles read Paulo's early works. Both men explained to their admirers how their ideas were similar and how they were different. The two actually talked with each other for the first time in 1973, when asked to participate in an adult education conference held in Chicago. They met again in similar circumstances in New York and California and at a conference in Nicaragua. But these meetings were for other people and other occasions, affording Myles and Paulo little opportunity to confirm what each had grown to believe about the other man and his ideas. However, when they met at a conference in California in the summer of 1987, the time had come for them to talk, to explore ideas, to get to know one another—*really* know each other. It was also time to let the world in on what each man, whose work was already well known, had to say to each other.

Paulo came to Los Angeles to participate in a conference in honor of his late wife, Elza. Myles was visiting his daughter there and was convalescing following an operation for colon cancer. Paulo asked him to consider "speaking a book." Paulo, as people familiar with his writings know, had used this method to get his own ideas into print. Myles, not known for publishing his own ideas, characteristically let go a hearty laugh, perhaps because he saw the irony of the situation, but more likely because he immediately felt the joy that such an experience would bring to both men. Others around them, including Sue Thrasher of Highlander, saw the historical possibilities, and went to work to bring the idea to fruition.

Brenda Bell knew of John Peters's interest in bringing Paulo to the University of Tennessee as a visiting scholar, and through Brenda he learned about Sue's desire to bring Paulo to Highlander. With the help of our colleagues at the university and at Highlander, financial arrangements were made, tentative travel plans and a schedule were laid on, and anticipation began to build.

Soon a small group of Highlander and university staff members began to meet and plan a week of events that would center around conversations between Paulo and Myles. The group planned symposia and classes at the university for students and faculty, and two meetings at Highlander for community activists and other friends of Highlander. Public demand for time with Paulo and Myles was great, but the planners managed to keep the main event intact, and the conversations began.

The clear, cool days in early December 1987 were generous to the mountains around Highlander, allowing participants to converse on the idyllic Highlander hilltop where Myles lived. Paulo particularly enjoyed occasionally gazing through the expansive window to the long, wide view beyond Myles's hearth. They could relax, explore their histories, and feel the texture and depth of each other's experiences as they grew closer as good friends. Their conversations soon became like a dance between old companions accustomed to the subtle leads and responses by one, then the other.

Members of the Highlander staff and friends occasionally participated in the conversation, tugging on the dialogue, sometimes clarifying a difference in ideas, sometimes netting an elusive thought in need of illustration, but never breaking the rhythm of the conversation. Myles, Paulo, and the "third party" conversationalists were recorded on audio tape, the tape was transcribed verbatim, and the long editing process began.

As editors, we have worked to give the conversations some structure and have presented them in a series of chapters that are very close to the order in which the themes emerged in the conversations. However, we tried to preserve the subtlety of each man's critique of the other's ideas, the immediacy of their dialogue, the occasional discontinuities in conversational themes, the spontaneity of their remarks, and the cognitive leaps revealed in their conversations. We wanted others to feel a part of this remarkable conversation, as we did when we read the transcripts, and to experience what Paulo frequently referred to as the "sensualism of reading, full of feelings, of emotions, of tastes."

The book is divided into six chapters, containing sections of conversation that focus on distinct topics. Each section is headed by a quote from the text, chosen by the editors to represent what follows and to retain the lyrical quality of the conversation itself. The book is perhaps best read as a series of conversations rather than a tightly structured whole.

The "Introduction" contains a discussion between Myles and Paulo about why they decided to speak a book and how they should go about it, setting the tone for several days of dialogue that followed. "Formative Years" is about their youth, their families, their cultural settings, and some of their early experiences, such as Myles's work in the Citizenship Schools. This chapter highlights the connection between the men's biographies and the nature of their experiences and practice.

The next chapter is about their ideas, many of which have been shared by Myles and Paulo in other places. For example, they consider whether education can be neutral, how the concept of authority fits into their thinking and practice, their view of charismatic leadership, and what they see as differences between educating and organizing. This chapter is richly spiced with stories and anecdotes. Many have been told before, but never as they unfold here in the interaction of the two storytellers.

In "Educational Practice," Myles and Paulo discuss specific features of their work in communities, workshops, and classrooms in a variety of cultural settings. They describe the role of the educator, intervention in the learning experiences of others, and the relationship of theory and practice in the context of adult learning. Again, this chapter is amply illustrated with stories and examples, most expressing common ground in the two men's experiences.

"Education and Social Change" is at once abstract and filled with concrete examples of the struggles of both men to change systems. Perhaps the clearest divergence of their views is illustrated here, when Paulo and Myles discuss the pros and cons of working from inside systems as opposed to effecting change from outside. Examples from Latin America and from North America illustrate the differences in cultural contexts that help account for their different thoughts and strategies.

The final chapter, "Reflections," is a look back to the people, literature, and events that influenced their thinking and their work. It includes a sweeping discussion of broader ideas and worldly matters. This chapter also captures much of what is brilliantly simple about the two men's thinking and how that thinking was shaped by more than one hundred years of combined educational practice.

Two years after the conversations took place, Myles and Paulo were reunited at Highlander, where Paulo came to review the manuscript draft and, sadly, to see Myles for the last time. Three days later Myles slipped into a coma. He died January 19, 1990. At their final meeting, Paulo and Myles were pleased that they had made this road together.

THE EDITORS

Acknowledgments

Preparations for the conversations and the development of this book was truly a group effort. Sue Thrasher, staff member at Highlander, did much of the early logistical work to get it all under way. Vickie Creed and Candie Carawan of the Highlander staff organized events at Highlander and worked with University of Tennessee staff in arranging events on campus. Sue Thrasher, John Gaventa, Helen Lewis, Vicki Creed, Linda Martin, Thorsten Horton, Mario Acevedo, and Candie Carawan all participated as third parties during the conversations between Myles and Paulo. Mike Lemonds assisted in the first stage of manuscript editing, and Becky Allen, Herb Kohl, and Colin Greer read early versions of the manuscript and gave their very helpful reactions. Wanda Chasteen, and Janie Bean laboriously typed transcripts from audio recordings. Mary

xiii

Nickell contributed considerable secretarial time during events leading to the conversations. Karen Jones and Loretta McHan provided secretarial assistance in the editing process. A number of community activists and friends of Highlander participated in a day-long workshop that helped stimulate parts of the conversations. Many other staff members and friends of Highlander shared their time and energies at different stages of the project, as did our own families and friends. Finally, most of the expenses associated with the activities and the manuscript preparation were paid by the University of Tennessee, the Board of Homeland Ministries of the United Church of Christ, and by the Myles and Zilphia Horton Fund of the Highlander Research and Education Center (to which all royalties from this book are being donated). On behalf of all people who will be touched by these conversations between Myles and Paulo, we deeply appreciate what those mentioned here contributed.

THE EDITORS

Editors' Introduction

*Myles Horton
and Paulo Freire:
Background
on the Men,
the Movements,
and the Meetings*

In December 1987, Myles Horton and Paulo Freire, two
pioneers of education for social change, came together
to "talk a book" about their experiences and ideas.
Though they came from different environments—one
from the rural mountains of Appalachia, the other from
São Paulo, the largest industrial city in Brazil—Myles
and Paulo shared a vision and a history of using participatory education as a crucible for empowerment of
the poor and powerless. Their remarkably common experiences represent more than one hundred years of
educational praxis.

In many ways, Myles and Paulo seem an unlikely
match. They began their work at different times. Horton started the Highlander Folk School on the Cumberland Plateau in Tennessee in 1932. Paulo began his
literacy programs in Recife in northeastern Brazil some

twenty-five years later. Paulo has always been more theoretical in his writing and discourse. Myles conversed more simply, often through anecdotes and storytelling drawn from his years of struggle. Paulo's work, at least initially, came from a position within a university. He continued it as a government official responsible for literacy programs throughout Brazil. Myles always worked outside university and government institutions, using as his base the Highlander Folk School (later the Highlander Research and Education Center), an independent center conducting adult education programs at the grass roots. Partly as a result of political circumstance—he was forced to flee from Brazil in 1964—Paulo has worked in many countries and is a more global figure. Myles too has faced political repercussions—especially the attacks, beatings, and investigations during the McCarthy era and civil rights movement—but chose (and was able) to stay rooted in one region of the southern United States for more than five decades.

One of the reasons that Paulo Freire wanted to "talk a book" with Myles, he often said, was that he was tired of North American audiences telling him that his ideas were only applicable to Third World conditions. "No," he said, "the story of Myles and of Highlander Center show that the ideas apply to the First World, too."

How could two men, working in such different social spaces and times, arrive at similar ideas and methods? Underlying the philosophy of both is the idea that knowledge grows from and is a reflection of social experience. It is important, therefore, that these conversations and the ideas of these two men also be linked to the social context from which they grew. Perhaps more important than their First World or Third World roots is the fact that both Myles and Paulo came from the poorest regions *within* their own countries, regions that shared many characteristics in their relationships to the larger political economy. Within that context, they also shared similarities of life history and of involvement in social movements that helped to shape their vision and their practice.

The Men

Myles Horton was born in 1905 in the western Tennessee Delta, an area whose history is based upon plantation agriculture, a slave-based economy, absentee ownership, and severe rural poverty. He founded the Highlander Folk School in Grundy County, Tennessee, one of the poorest Appalachian counties and an area dominated by powerful coal interests. During the 1930s, at the time of Highlander's founding, the region was being swept by industrialization. Myles and Highlander started their programs with rural workers, who were being displaced from the land and driven into the textile mills, mines, and factories as part of the "development" of the rural South.

Paulo Freire was born in 1921 in Recife, in northeast Brazil, one of Brazil's poorest regions. As Appalachia and the rural South have been in the United States, the region has been plagued with "poverty, hunger and illiteracy for many years. . . . The northeast has Brazil's highest birthrate, shortest life expectancy rates, severest malnutrition, lowest literacy rates, and highest levels of unemployment and underemployment."[1] There are other common characteristics between the two regions. The rural areas of northeast Brazil were dominated by sugar estates and slave and peasant labor, not dissimilar to the cotton plantation economy of the South. Industrialization and "development" schemes transformed the rural-based economy, leading peasants to migrate from the countryside to the towns and cities such as Recife. Both regions were dependent upon powerful economic interests, initially the plantation owners and later the multinationals, and were characterized by sharp dichotomies between rich and poor, powerful and powerless.

Myles and Paulo also experienced rather similar family backgrounds. Both were born of parents who were slightly more educated and well-to-do than many of the poor around them. But in both families, the broader economic changes were to lead to personal adversity.

Myles's father and mother, who had been through grammar school, were schoolteachers. They later lost their jobs when teachers were required to have certification. Myles's father survived as he could, spending time as a day laborer, a clerk, and then a sharecropper. Myles recalls: "I can remember very well that I never felt sorry for myself. I just accepted the fact that those were the conditions, and that I was a victim of those conditions, but I never had a feeling of inferiority to people. I think that I got that from my parents too, because even though they were struggling and poor, they never accepted the fact that they were inferior to anybody or that anybody was inferior to them."

Paulo's father was a low-level officer in the military where "pay was low, but the prestige was high."[2] During the Depression, his father lost that job, as Myles's father had lost his, and the family left Recife for the nearby town of Jabotão. There, Paulo says, "I had the possibility to experience hunger. And I say I had the *possibility* because I think that experience was very useful to me."

Though Myles's and Paulo's parents were constantly on the edge of poverty, struggling to make ends meet, they were strongly supportive of schooling for their children. Paulo recalls his father teaching him to read "under a mango tree," while Myles describes loving books and reading anything that he could borrow from neighbors, friends, and relatives in the nearest little town, named, coincidentally, Brazil! Through family friends or other contacts, both sets of parents were able to send their sons to nearby towns for high school when they were 15 or 16 years old. Conforming to the schooling system was not easy for either boy, even at a young age. As a child, Paulo was thought to have learning problems, leading his teachers to label him as having a "mild mental retardation."[3] Myles describes how he hated to do the rote work that was required and instead would sneakily read other books, leading him to "get in trouble for reading in school."

Unlike many of their friends from similar circumstances, both Myles and Paulo attended college, Myles in a small Tennessee school called Cumberland Presbyterian, Paulo in the University of Recife, where he was trained as a lawyer, a profession he quickly gave up. Both were drawn to the social aspects of Christianity, among other early intellectual influences. Myles went on from college to Union Seminary in the late 1920s, where he was influenced by Reinhold Niebuhr, the Christian socialist and social critic. He also went on to study sociology briefly at the University of Chicago, where he worked with Jane Addams in the Settlement House movement.

Freire, too, was highly influenced by a growing Catholic Action movement, which was to lay the ground for what would later become known as the liberation theology movement. As a student, he joined a Catholic Action group at the university, which, unlike most of the church, was "more preoccupied with the concept of society and social change, and acutely aware of the conditions of poverty and hunger in the Northeast."[4] While Myles moved away from his theological roots, Freire continued to be active in and deeply influenced by the radical Catholic movement.[5]

Myles and Paulo were shaped as well by their own families and personal relationships, especially their wives. In 1935 Myles married Zilphia Mae Johnson, a talented musician and singer, who contributed to Highlander and Myles an understanding of the role that music and culture could play in nurturing social change.[6] In 1943, Paulo married Elza Maria Costa de Oliveira, whom he credits for constantly helping him develop his educational ideas and method. Myles suffered personal tragedy when Zilphia died in 1956. Elza died in 1987, before Paulo visited Highlander to hold these conversations. Both Myles and Paulo remarried: Myles to Aimee Isgrig, who worked on the staff with Myles and wrote a dissertation on Highlander;[7] Paulo to Anna Maria Araujo, one of his students who wrote her dissertation with him on the history of illiteracy in Brazil.[8]

While Myles and Paulo shared these commonalities in family background, they chose very different paths to begin their educational work.

After leaving graduate school in sociology at the University of Chicago, Myles went to Denmark to study the Danish Folk High School movement, hoping to gain insights for his own fledgling idea of a community school in the United States. There he learned more about the ideas of Bishop Grundtvig, founder of the movement—ideas such as the importance of peer learning in nonformal settings free from government regulation. In Copenhagen on Christmas night 1931, he wrote of his dream of beginning a school in the mountains of Tennessee:

I can't sleep, but there are dreams. What you must do is go back, get a simple place, move in and you are there. The situation is there. You start with this and you let it grow. You know your goal. It will build its own structure and take its own form.

xxi

You can go to school all your life, you'll never figure it out because you are trying to get an answer that can only come from the people in the life situation.[9]

With this vision in mind, he returned to Tennessee in 1932, and along with Don West started the Highlander Folk School. Though he took short stints away from Highlander to develop educational programs for unions, Myles was to serve as director of Highlander the next forty years, until he retired in 1972.

After abandoning law, Paulo Freire began work in 1946 at a social service agency for the state of Pernambuco. He was responsible for programs of education for the rural poor and industrial workers in the area that included Recife. Here he first became interested in the problems of adult literacy and popular education, and he began to read and develop his ideas. In 1954 he resigned this post and began teaching history and philosophy of education at the University of Recife. In 1959, with the election of a new, progressive mayor in Recife, Freire was placed in charge of the Movimento de Cultura Popular (MCP), an active adult-education program. (At the same time, he obtained his doctorate from the University of Recife, where in his thesis he outlined his emerging adult-education ideas.) In 1962, he was named head of a new cultural extension service established for popular education in the region. And following a change in national government and a victory by João Goulart, Freire, whose methods were by now becoming well-known, was asked in 1963 to head the National Literacy Program of the Brazilian Minis-

try of Education and Culture—the post that was to lead
to his exile in 1964.

The Movements

Thus, Myles's and Paulo's ideas were to develop through
two very different forms of praxis—Myles's from a
small, independent residential education center situ-
ated outside the formal schooling system or the state,
Paulo from within university and state-sponsored programs. Their ideas were to converge not through a
series of theoretical deductions but through their interaction with the social context and their involvement
with broader popular struggles for participation and
freedom. Though both are often credited for what they
contributed to these movements, perhaps more significant is the way in which their careers were in fact shaped
by social movements themselves.

When Myles and others founded Highlander on
the Cumberland Plateau in 1932, they had a vision of
change but no clear idea of the movement that was
to bring it about. Their intent was simply "to provide
an educational center in the South for the training of
rural and industrial leaders, and for the conservation
and enrichment of the indigenous cultural values of the
mountains." [10] The school's first fund-raising letter, sent
by Reinhold Niebuhr, stated that the school proposed
"to use education as one of the instruments for bringing about a new social order." [11] The seeds of the idea
settled on the fertile soil of industrialization that was

sweeping the rural South, bringing with it the demands for economic justice for southern workers. Highlander staff members quickly provided assistance to workers and used these experiences to shape their educational ideas. During one strike, following meetings with coal miners in Wilder, Tennessee, Myles was arrested by the National Guard and charged with "coming here, getting information, going back and teaching it."[12] By the 1940s Highlander had become a residential education center for the Congress for Industrial Organizations (CIO), providing schools for union leaders from around the South.

In the early 1950s, feeling that racial justice must accompany economic justice, Highlander shifted its attention to the problem of desegregation in the South. For the next decade it was a meeting and educational ground for the emerging civil rights movement. Dozens of meetings and workshops at Highlander were followed by civil rights activities that were to make major changes in race relations in the United States. Rosa Parks, who had been to Highlander only a few months before, sparked the Montgomery Bus Boycott when she refused to give up her seat on a bus to a white man. The boycott in turn gave rise to the leadership of Martin Luther King, Jr., also a visitor to Highlander and a colleague of Horton's.

In the early days of the civil rights movement, one of Highlander's most influential programs was the development of Citizenship Schools. Begun in Johns Island, South Carolina, in response to a request from Esau Jenkins, a black community leader, the Citizenship Schools taught blacks how to read and write in order to gain the vote and political power. In so doing, they also developed principles of literacy education that used popular black leaders as teachers and taught reading based on the students' needs and desires to gain freedom. In the 1960s, leadership of the highly successful program was passed to the Southern Christian Leadership Conference (SCLC). By 1970 SCLC estimated that approximately one hundred thousand blacks had learned to read and write through the Citizenship Schools.[13]

In his book, *The Origins of the Civil Rights Movement*, Aldon Morris traces this link between the Citizenship Schools and the mobilization of the civil rights movement. He argues that "the citizenship schools were probably the most profound contribution of all those made to the emerging civil rights movement" by "movement halfway houses" such as Highlander.[14] (The Citizenship Schools are discussed extensively by Horton and Freire in Chapter 2 of this book.)

Freire's ideas found a similar base in the movements for democratic education in northeast Brazil. During the growth of these movements in the late 1950s, the traditional social structure was changing, the dependence on the sugar plantation economy was declining, and industrialization was occurring at a rapid rate. With the emergence of a populist reformist government of Pernambuco, the Northeast of Brazil became a laboratory for the emergence of new demands for participation by the people in their own development. Two movements in particular formed the setting for the literacy and popular education program of which Freire was a part. One was the growth of rural trade unions or peasant associations known as Peasant Leagues. By 1960 an estimated eighty thousand workers belonged to these leagues in the Northeast. Among their demands, in addition to the right to organize cooperatives for a program of land reform, was the right for illiterates to vote, a right that was denied to the peasants at the time. The second movement grew from Catholic activists and included the Basic Education Movement, or MEB (Movimento Educacão de Base), and radical Catholic groups such as Popular Action and Catholic University Youth (to which Freire had belonged).

In 1959 Miguel Arraes, a nationalist and radical democrat, was elected mayor of Recife. Hoping to bring about fundamental changes in the constitution, he knew that he would have to bring education to the rural poor, who represented a majority of the population but could not vote because they were largely illiterate. He formed the Recife Popular Culture Movement, or MCP (Movimento Cultural Popular), which would carry out a program of grassroots education, adult literacy, and development of critical consciousness of the masses. Doing so would help to mobilize the peasants to exercise their political power, and Freire was asked to head this program. Here he developed culture centers and culture circles that were at the heart of the literacy education process. Recife and the surrounding area thus became the microcosm for the development of Freire's ideas, ideas that were deeply related to the popular demands and political movements of the time.

The period was one of great awakening and change

throughout the country. "Different forces were in motion and the process was an irreversible one. It was the breaking of an old society and the emergence of a more democratic, pluralistic social order." [15] With the election of a new populist national government in 1960, a variety of popular education and culture programs were initiated. Freire was appointed head of the new National Literacy Program. Under the National Literacy Plan of 1964, his methods were to be extended to reach 5 million illiterate people throughout the country. The MEB, the Catholic Church's own national adult education organization, also adopted Freire's methods.

The plans were not fully realized. In 1964 a military coup overthrew the Goulart government. The National Literacy Campaign was halted. The government enacted new laws, "which deprived one hundred influential members of the previous government their rights for a decade." [16] Among them was Paulo Freire, who was forced to flee the country along with hundreds of other activists and leaders in the government.

For both Freire and Horton, the linking of literacy and enfranchisement posed a major threat to long-entrenched power structures, a threat that led to repercussions. As Freire has pointed out:

It was so extraordinary, that it couldn't be allowed to continue. In a state like Pernambuco, which at the time had about 800 thousand voters, it would be possible in one year to have up to 1 million and 300 thousand new voters. . . . Well, that had too great a repercussion on the prevalent power structure. It was too risky a game for the dominant class. [17]

xxvii

In Brazil, the Rio de Janeiro newspaper *El Globo* accused Freire of "spreading foreign ideas throughout the country."[18] Freire was arrested, jailed for seventy-five days and interrogated for eighty-three hours. The military government declared him an "international subversive, a traitor to Christ and to the people of Brazil besides being an absolute ignoramus and illiterate."[19]

Similarly, as Highlander emerged as a key force in the empowerment of blacks in the South, it came under attack. The southern white power structure attempted to use the virulent anticommunist rhetoric of the McCarthy period to discredit Horton and the school. In 1954, Horton was investigated by Senator James Eastland, a wealthy Mississippi planter and white supremacist, for his alleged communist connections. In another celebrated incident, Georgia's segregationist governor, Marvin Griffin, dispatched infiltrators to the celebration of Highlander's twenty-fifth anniversary in 1957, where Martin Luther King, Jr., was the keynote speaker. Pictures were taken of King, Horton, and others, turned into billboards, and plastered around the South with the label, "King at a Communist Training School." In 1959 the Highlander Folk School was raided by the State of Tennessee and its property and assets seized.[20] Arguing that you could padlock the school but not the idea, Horton renamed it the Highlander Research and Education Center and moved it to Knoxville—and later to New Market, where it is today.

Despite the adversity, both men displayed the optimism that underlies much of their educational beliefs. The attacks, while imposing great personal costs, became learning grounds for further activities. After a brief stint in Bolivia (until another coup), Freire went on to Chile, where he assisted in developing educational programs on behalf of agrarian reform. From there he went to Harvard, where he wrote and lectured. His ideas began to receive much more international attention, especially following the publication of *Pedagogy of the Oppressed* in English in 1975.[21] In 1970, he joined the World Council of Churches in Geneva. He continued to travel, assist in the development of programs, and write until he was able to return to Brazil in 1980.

As the North American civil rights movement began to grow in the mid-1960s, the Citizenship Schools became incorporated under the Southern Christian Leadership Conference. Myles tried to continue developing educational programs in other parts of Appalachia and the South. Later, passing on leadership of the Highlander Research and Education Center to younger associates, he focused on traveling, speaking, and conducting workshops in the United States and abroad. Today, the center continues its work throughout Appalachia and the South. While issues have changed—today they include environmental abuse, poverty and economic justice, youth empowerment, leadership development —the philosophy of education for empowerment remains.

The Meetings

Given their backgrounds, it was perhaps inevitable that Horton and Freire would meet. When they did come together in Myles's home at Highlander, it was an important time for both. Earlier in the year Paulo's wife, Elza, had died, and Paulo was still in a state of sorrow and depression. Myles had recovered from an operation for colon cancer in the summer, and though he was doing well, he was clearly concerned about how to share his ideas while he was able.

In this book, the two men link their own lives, their ideas on radical education, and their experiences in a fresh way. After reading the edited manuscript, Paulo would say that of all the themes that he and Myles discussed, two underlying ideas are the most important. First is the fundamental belief in the importance of the freedom of people everywhere, the struggle for which is widely seen as the 1990s open—in Brazil, in Eastern Europe, in the Soviet Union, in southern Africa. Second is the radical democratic belief in the capacity and right of all people to achieve that freedom through self-emancipation.

Both men believe, then, real liberation is achieved through popular participation. Participation in turn is realized through an educational practice that itself is both liberatory and participatory, that simultaneously creates a new society and involves the people themselves in the creation of their own knowledge.

Most important for Myles and Paulo, these ideas are not abstractions, but grow from their struggles to link theory and practice in their own lives. In turn, their discussions illuminate questions faced by educators and activists around the world who are concerned with linking participatory education to liberation and social change. What is the role of the teacher? The organizer? The educator? How is education linked to mobilization and culture to create a new society? Can society be transformed by education, or must education itself first be transformed? Is there space for liberatory education within the state-sponsored educational system, as Paulo tried to show, or must change come from somewhere outside, such as Myles's Highlander?

In dealing with these themes, the conversations give us, as Henry Giroux has said of Freire, both a "language of critique" of existing power relations and a "language of possibility" for creating a new society through a new educational and social practice.[22]

The process of "talking a book" became for the two men intensely personal. They not only deepened their critique of knowledge and power but also developed and renewed their own strength. Over the course of their conversations, they shared a respect and personal affection for one another in a way that gave each a new sense of possibility and hope.

Paulo credits his reflections with Myles as helping to bring him out of his despair over Elza's death. In his meeting with Myles in December 1987, he saw in Myles a man sixteen years his senior—then 82 years old—still full of energy and vision. He says, "At Highlander I began to read and to write again." He also was drawn back into the struggles for popular participation in Brazil. When a popular socialist candidate was elected mayor of São Paulo in 1988, Paulo became Secretary for Education and took up the new challenge of transforming a traditional educational system in Latin America's largest and most industrialized city.

In the winter of 1989, in the first popular elections in twenty-nine years, Paulo supported Luis Inacio Lula da Silva, known as Lula, a trade unionist for the Workers Party (PT), who came very close to winning the national elections. Had he done so, it would have been a new historical moment in Brazilian politics, and Paulo Freire would again have been named Minister of Education for the whole country, the post he held when he was exiled in 1964. "Tell Myles that I may not be able to see him in January," Freire told us as we tried to arrange the final meeting. "Tell him that I may be in power."

"That," Horton allowed, "would be a reasonable excuse."

Lula came very close to winning the election, but not close enough. In early January 1990, following Lula's defeat, Paulo and Anita, his second wife, came to Highlander for a final review of the manuscript and, it would turn out, a final meeting with Myles. In the fall of 1989, Myles had undergone surgery for a tumor in the brain, two years after his initial bout with colon cancer. As his mental and physical strength slipped away, he focused on rereading the edited transcript and on the possibility of another meeting with Freire for final changes. By this second meeting, another tumor had formed in Myles's brain, and he worried about being alert enough to discuss the manuscript with Paulo. He rallied for the meeting. The two men were able to have several brief conversations, to concur that the manuscript was almost ready, and to express their pleasure with it. As they talked and ate together in Myles's home, the atmosphere was one of intense emotion. Looking out over the mountains and at the birds at the feeder, Paulo would comment: "It is sad, but dying is a necessary part of living. It is wonderful that Myles may die here. Dying here is dying in the midst of life."

Three days after his last visit with Paulo and Anita, Myles Horton slipped into a coma. He died a week later. He was 84 years old. "It is incredible," said Paulo, "that at the moment that Myles dies, I assume the responsibility of leading the public system of education in São Paulo. . . . It was an honor for me to participate with him. He's an incredible man. The history of this man, his individual presence in the world, is something which *justifies* the world." Were he able, Myles, we are sure, would say the same of Paulo.

NOTES

1   Carroll L. Wessinger, *Parallel Characteristics: Northeast Brazil/Appalachia* (Philadelphia: Lutheran Church of America, n.d.), 6.

2   Jorge Jeria, "Vagabond of the Obvious: A Bibliography of Paulo Freire," *Vitae Scholasticae: The Bulletin of Educational Biography* 5, nos. 1–2 (1986): 4.

3   Jeria, "Vagabond," 9, quoting "Background on Paulo Freire," *Convergence* 6, no. 1 (1973): 46.

4   Jeria, "Vagabond," 13.

5   Emanuel de Kadt, *Catholic Radicals in Brazil* (London: Oxford University Press, 1970), 102–5.

6   Zilphia Horton is often credited with helping to record and adapt the song "We Shall Overcome," which was brought to Highlander by a group of tobacco workers in the late 1940s and was later spread to the civil rights movement by Guy Carawan, Pete Seeger, and others.

7   The dissertation has been published as Aimee Isgrig Horton, *The Highlander Folk School: A History of Its Major Programs, 1932–1961* (Brooklyn, N.Y.: Carlson, 1989).

8   Anna Maria Araujo, *Analfabetismo No Brasil* (São Paulo: INEP, 1989).

9   Quoted by John M. Peters and Brenda Bell, "Horton of Highlander," in Peter Jarvis, ed., *Twentieth Century Thinkers in Adult Education* (London: Croom Helm, 1987), 243.

10   Quoted in Peters and Bell, "Horton of Highlander," 250.

11   Ibid.

12   See Frank Adams, "Highlander Folk School: Getting Information, Going Back and Teaching It," *Harvard Education Review* 42, no. 4 (1972): 497–520.

13   Bell and Peters, "Horton of Highlander," citing Adams, "Highlander Folk School."

14   Aldon D. Morris, *Origins of the Civil Rights Movement: Black Communities Organizing for Change* (New York: Free Press, 1984), 149.

15   Jeria, "Vagabond," 33.

16   Ibid., 45.

17   "Paulo Freire no exilioficou mais brasileiro ainda," *Pasquim* (Rio de Janeiro), no. 462 (5 and 11 May 1978), quoted in Vivian Von Schelling, "Culture and Underdevelopment in Brazil with Particular Reference to Mario de Andrade and Paulo Freire" (Ph.D. thesis, University of Sussex, 1984), 265.

18   Jeria, "Vagabond," 44, quoting accounts of T. Skidmore, *The*

Politics of Brazil, 1930–1964 (New York: Oxford University Press, 1967), 406.

19 Jeria, "Vagabond," 48, quoting accounts of Marcio Moreira, *A Grain of Mustard Seed: The Awakening of the Brazilian Revolution* (New York: Anchor, 1973), 115.

20 There are many accounts of these attacks on Highlander. See especially John M. Glen, *Highlander: No Ordinary School 1932–1962*, (Lexington: University Press of Kentucky, 1988).

21 Available in a number of editions and languages, the book has sold over two hundred thousand copies.

22 Henry A. Giroux, "Introduction," in Paulo Freire, *The Politics of Education: Culture, Power, and Liberation* (South Hadley, Mass.: Bergin & Garvey, 1985).

SELECTED BIBLIOGRAPHY

PAULO FREIRE

Freire, Paulo. *Cultural Action for Freedom.* Harmondsworth, Eng.: Penguin, 1972.

––––––. *Education as the Practice of Liberty.* New York: McGraw Hill, 1973.

––––––. *Education for Critical Consciousness.* New York: Continuum, 1981.

––––––. *Education: The Practice of Liberty.* London: Writers and Readers Publishing, 1976. (Originally published in the U.K. as *Education for Critical Consciousness.*)

––––––. *Pedagogy in Process: The Letters to Guinea Bissau.* Translated by Carmen St. John Hunter. New York: Seabury Press, 1978.

––––––. *Pedagogy of the Oppressed.* New York: Seabury Press, 1970.

––––––. *The Politics of Education: Culture, Power, and Liberation.* South Hadley, Mass.: Bergin & Garvey, 1985.

Freire, Paulo, with Donald Macedo. *Literacy: Reading the Word and the World*. South Hadley, Mass.: Bergin & Garvey, 1987.

Grabowski, K. *Paulo Freire: A Revolutionary Dilemma for the Adult Educator*. Syracuse, N.Y.: Syracuse University Press, 1972.

Jeria, Jorge. "Vagabond of the Obvious: A Bibliography of Paulo Freire." *Vitae Scholasticae* 5, nos. 1–2 (1986): 1–75.

Mackie, Robert. *Literacy and Revolution: The Pedagogy of Paulo Freire*. New York: Continuum, 1981. Also published by Pluto Press, London.

Shor, Ira. *A Pedagogy for Liberation: Dialogues on Transforming Education*. South Hadley, Mass.: Bergin & Garvey, 1987.

MYLES HORTON

Adams, Frank. "Highlander Folk School: Getting Information, Going Back and Teaching It." *Harvard Educational Review* 42, no. 4 (1972): 497–520.

Adams, Frank, with Myles Horton. *Unearthing Seeds of Fire: The Idea of Highlander*. Winston-Salem, N.C.: John F. Blair, 1975.

Clark, Septima, with Cynthia Brown, ed. *Ready from Within: Septima Clark and the Civil Rights Movement*. Navarro, Calif.: Wild Tree, 1986.

Glen, John M. *Highlander: No Ordinary School, 1932–1962*. Lexington: University Press of Kentucky, 1988.

Horton, Aimee Isgrig. *The Highlander Folk School: A History of its Major Programs, 1932–1961*. Brooklyn, N.Y.: Carlson, 1989.

Horton, Myles. "Influences on Highlander Research and Education Center." Pp. 17–31 in Det Danske Selskab, *Grundtvig's Ideas in North America—Influences and Parallels*. Copenhagen: Det Danske Selskab, 1983.

Horton, Myles, with Herbert and Judith Kohl. *The Long Haul*. New York: Doubleday Books, 1990.

Horton, Myles, with Bill Moyers. "The Adventures of a Radical Hillbilly." *Bill Moyers' Journal*. Originally broadcast on WNET, New York, June 5, 1981.

Kennedy, William Bean. "Highlander Praxis: Learning with Myles Horton." *Teachers College Record* (Fall 1981): 105–19.

Morris, Aldon D. *Origins of the Civil Rights Movement: Black Communities Organizing for Change*. New York: Free Press, 1984.

Peters, John M. and Brenda Bell. "Horton of Highlander." In Peter Jarvis, ed., *Twentieth Century Thinkers in Adult Education*. London: Croom Helm, 1987.

Phenix, Lucy Massie (producer). *You Got to Move: Stories of Change in the South*. New York: Icarus Films, 1985.

Tjerandsen, Carl. *Education for Citizenship: A Foundation's Experience*. Santa Cruz, Calif.: Emil Schwarzhaupt Foundation, 1980.

———. "The Highlander Heritage: Education for Social Change." *Convergence* 15, no. 6 (1983): 10–22.

WE MAKE THE ROAD BY WALKING

Candie Carawan

CHAPTER 1

Introduction

"We make the road by walking"

PAULO: What is beautiful is how we look alike, Myles and I.
Here we are among friends, so I can say that. I can
talk about how I look like Myles—being Paulo Freire,
a Brazilian with a different context—about the ways I
find myself in his thought and in our conversations in
this book.

In July 1987, when Myles and I met together in Los
Angeles at the symposium in memory of Elza Freire, I
had a dream; I thought it would be interesting to try
to speak a book with him. I asked Myles to do this with
me, and he laughed! But we agreed.

It's as if I were starting everything now, talking with
Myles. This is the beginning of a different time in my
life. After Elza's death, after the death of my wife of
forty-two years, I am making a fantastic effort to con-

3

tinue to be who I was before she died and also to be a different person, because without her I discovered I am no longer the first person. It's not possible to be myself without her. So necessarily I have to be different, but you understand. . . . You see, I'm trying to renew myself, and talking with Myles, trying to "speak a book" with him, is for me one of the most important dimensions of this second phase, or last time, of my life, which I hope will be long!

MYLES: One reason that doing this with you is important to me, Paulo, is that people will profit from our conversation because they probably have the same kinds of questions that we have for each other. This type of conversation hasn't been possible before because even though we've been together on a number of occasions, the format is that others ask us questions. We never have the chance to ask each other questions. This is a good opportunity for us!

PAULO: Let me tell you how I have worked in situations like this. I started doing this with other friends of mine, other educators, in Brazil, maybe five years ago. I called it "spoken books." Instead of writing a book, we speak the book, and afterwards others can transcribe it, but first we have the order of the spoken words. This should give us a duality in the conversation, a certain relaxation, a result of losing seriousness in thinking while talking. The purpose is to have a good conversation but in the sort of style that makes it easier to read the words.

In this book we can capture this movement of conversation. The reader goes and comes with the movement of the conversation. I don't want to loose even one expression of Myles. Every time I don't understand, I will ask Myles to stop, and one of you can tell me again, but not in Myles's accent!

MYLES: Sometimes I've seen you switch to Portuguese because you can think better in Portuguese. I can think better the way I talk, too.

PAULO: Of course. You must do that because it is very good. I would be speaking Portuguese also if you could understand. It's better for me. I don't want to lose anything of your free expression.

MYLES: I can do it my way, but you can't do it your way because we don't have any facilities to translate.

PAULO: Myles, I think we could start our conversation by saying something to each other about our very existence in the world. We should not start, for example, speaking about the objectives of education. Do you see that this is not for me? You could speak a little bit about your life and work, and I will say something about my life. Then we could interact in some moments of the conversation, as a starting point.

Afterward, I think we could begin to touch some issues in general—education, popular education, politics of education. This is how I am thinking about issues in order to organize chapters as we do when we write. Instead of that, we begin to create factual issues without localizing them in categories or pages, chapters. A strong central phrase from the dialogue can help readers begin to grasp some of the main issues of the conversation. How do you react to this?

MYLES: I like the way you are outlining our project. This is the first time I've understood what you had in mind.

But I did know enough to say that it wouldn't work for me to stick to topics or subjects. I wouldn't do it that way.

PAULO: It's very important for Brazilian readers to have information about Myles. About me, they have already, but about Myles they don't have and it's very, very important.

MYLES: Yes, but the people in this country need the same thing about you.

PAULO: Same thing, yes, of course. I would say the younger generations need to grab information while we're around, because the lack of historical memory is fantastic. There is a generation in Brazil who knows me. The next one, maybe no. And the next one will need a new edition of the book.

MYLES: Well now, when we talk about this kind of background, it's mainly the things that would help people understand where I came from in terms of my ideas and my thinking, what they are rooted in. Is that the idea?

PAULO: Yes. Everything you recognize as something important. I think that even though we need to have some outline, *I am sure that we make the road by walking.** It has to do with this house [Highlander], with this experience here. You're saying that in order to start, it should be necessary to start.

MYLES: I've never figured out any other way to start.

PAULO: The question for me is how is it possible for us, in

---

* The phrase "we make the road by walking" is an adaptation of a proverb by the Spanish poet Antonio Machado, in which one line reads "se hace camino al andar," or "you make the way as you go." See Antonio Machado, *Selected Poems*, trans. Alan S. Trueblood (Cambridge: Harvard University Press, 1982), 143.

6

the process of making the road, to be clear and to clarify our *own* making of the road. That is, then, to clarify some theoretical issues about education in the big vision of education. It's necessary. But I am not worried not to have now the list of these issues because I think that they will come out of the conversation.

MYLES: Not knowing what you had in mind, Paulo, I've been thinking about some of the things I'd like not so much to get into the book but to get out of this conversation—learning, just for my own enlightenment. And so I jotted down a lot of questions. I'd like to get your reaction. There will be a lot of questions in the back of my mind as we go through this conversation. Where it seems appropriate, I will be wanting to get your reaction to some of these things, how you deal with certain problems. For example, you've had a lot more experience with the academicians than I have. Then I'd like to get your reaction to our citizenship schools. These are just things that will be worked in as we go along. I'll take advantage of this to get a lot of things into the discussion.

I see this thing as just unfolding as we go along. I don't see any problem with that. I agree with Paulo; it's a natural way of doing it. It's what grows out of what you do. Everything comes out of the past and goes beyond. The conversation should be rooted and just keep moving along. I think we'll run out of time before we run out of ideas.

PAULO: Yes. As we are talking, I am beginning to think, for example, that maybe we could use even this first part of the conversation, in which we are talking about how to speak the book.

MYLES: I think what we've talked about here could be helpful to people to know. A book shouldn't be a mystery. It shouldn't be this business of separating books from life instead of having them reflect life.

PAULO: Here we are trying to decide how to get moments of each other's lives and to bring them into a book, a book which does not lose the essence of life. A dialogue is as the life that comes from the earth's springs. It is as if the book's life were doing that and being transformed into words, written words through our speaking, and afterward the speech comes into written speech, but it loses some of the power of life.

MYLES: I agree that this spoken way of doing it for me is the only way I can really do it. When I sit down to write and think things out, it gets kind of lifeless. A creative writer wouldn't have that problem, but I do. That's why I welcome this idea.

CHAPTER 2

Formative Years

"I was always getting in trouble for reading in school"

PAULO: I would start this new moment of our experience by asking you to say something about your life. How did you come into this beautiful practice we have here at Highlander? Tell us something about your life.

MYLES: Well I've always kind of shied away from an auto-biography because I always thought of myself as work-ing much more closely with other people than doing an individualistic sort of thing. I think people tend to look for a kind of a self-portrait in an autobiography. I don't find that so useful, reading about other people if they seem to appear to be doing it all by themselves.

PAULO: But Myles, do you know how I see that? First of all I recognize that your experience is a social experience. In fact, we cannot be explained by what we individu-ally do, but undoubtedly there is a certain individual

9

dimension of the social realization. You see? That is, there is something in Myles Horton who is just Myles Horton. There is not another Myles in the world, just yourself, as well as all of us here.

MYLES: Everybody's that way.

PAULO: Everybody's that way. It is in this way that I ask the question because I am curious about how the individual dimension of the social being, Myles, works inside of this social and historical context.

MYLES: I believe in another frame of reference. When I talk about Highlander and my experiences at Highlander, people forget that at the time I was having those experiences and having those influences on Highlander, there were other staff members also doing the same thing. I can only tell the way it looked from my perspective. It gives the impression that there were no other perspectives.

PAULO: Yes.

MYLES: That's the hesitancy I have, so I would hope to be able to kind of avoid that. And the other thing I would hope to do would be to make it clear that my ideas have changed and are constantly changing and *should* change and that I'm as proud of my inconsistencies as I am my consistencies. So I'd just like to shy away from the idea that somehow I've had these ideas and they've had such and such an effect.

I remember one time I was discussing Highlander with Robert Lynd, a sociologist who wrote *Middletown*. Bob said, "Myles, you tell a whole different story from what you told three or four years ago when I first met you." And I said, "Well sure, I'm a different person in different situations. I haven't stopped learning because I'm no longer in school." Lynd said, "You'll never be satisfied. You are the perfect example of somebody who sees a mountain, who says this is my goal and it's an almost impossible goal, and yet says I'm going to climb that mountain. I'm going to dedicate everything I've got, my life and everything, to achieving that goal. When this person gets up on top of that mountain and sees that it's not as high as the next mountain, he says well, this is not such hot stuff; it's not such a challenge. I'm going to try *that* mountain." Lynd said, "You'll never end; when mountains run out you'll imagine them." I have no objection to that!

PAULO: On the contrary. It would be very sad.

MYLES: Wait three or four years, and I'll be thinking something else. But there's a consistency in the sense that the direction is the same.

PAULO: I agree with you. This is for me! I think that one of the best ways for us to work as human beings is not only to know that we are uncompleted beings but to *assume* the uncompleteness. There is a little difference between knowing intellectually that we are unfinished and assuming the nature of being unfinished. We are not complete. We have to become inserted in a permanent process of searching. Without this we would die in life. It means that keeping curiosity is absolutely indispensable for us to continue to be or to become. This is what you said before. Fortunately you change, because it should be very sad if now you did not know that you will change, but just assumed that you *might* change. It is fantastic.

THIRD PARTY: How did you learn that, Myles, and also Paulo? Both of you have been teaching all your lives, trying to make other people restless and to learn never to give up the curiosity. What made *you* end up that way?

MYLES: Well, I know exactly where I was born because a few years ago an FBI agent came by and said in kind of an embarrassed way, "If you ever have any need to prove that you were born in the United States, why the FBI has a record. I was sent down to find out whether or not you were an American citizen, and I found the cabin in which you were born, and I found people who remember when you were born, so you were born here." I thanked him because I had told him I was always under the impression that I was born there!

The place he visited was a little place called Paulk's Mill right outside of Savannah, Tennessee, down the Tennessee River in a misplaced part of Appalachia. Tennessee has a basin and the central part of Tennessee is rimmed with mountains in the east and foothills in the west and south. Paulk's Mill was in the western foothills section down on the Tennessee River. My people on the Horton side had originally come from Watauga settlement in east Tennessee, from Elizabethton, not very far from here. My mother's people were Scottish. They'd come from North Carolina soon after the Revolutionary War. They got a land grant there for service in the revolutionary army.

By the time I came along back in 1905, my father

and mother, who had been through grammar school, were schoolteachers. Of course, at that time there were so few people with advanced education that when they started trying to get teachers for the primary schools they had to employ people who had had just a little bit more education. Something like popular education in Nicaragua; they had a little bit more education than the people they were teaching. That's important because I think that's probably the basis of my interest in education, having parents who were teachers to start with. Before I was school age, they were no longer teachers because the requirements had increased to where you had to have one year high-school education before you could teach. They couldn't afford to go back to school and get that education; therefore they had to stop teaching. But that interest stayed on.

My father was out of work for a while and took all kinds of odd jobs, manual labor jobs. Then he got into local politics and became a county official, a circuit court clerk. The reason he got elected to that office was that he was one of the few people in the county who could write legibly—which I never learned to do! The county kept all the records in longhand, and his qualification was he could write. Later on when more people learned to write, he lost his job, and then he was a day laborer for a while. Worked as a salesman. Learned to fix sewing machines and tried to figure out all kinds of ways to make a living. My first real memories of what I now know as poverty—at that time I didn't know it was poverty, I just thought that was the way people lived—

was when we were trying to raise cotton as sharecroppers out in the western part of Tennessee, where there was a lot of flat land. The nearest school was at the town of Brazil.

PAULO: Brazil, that's very interesting!

MYLES: I went through the ninth grade at Brazil, so part of my education was in Brazil!

When I went to eighth grade, that was the top grade. Three of us were ready for the ninth grade, so they got a teacher for the ninth grade in the school. She had just been to about the tenth or eleventh grade. I didn't have much help from teachers there, and I had to improvise a lot, had to make do with whatever resources were around, which didn't include books because they didn't have any books in the library. Even before that year ended, I realized that I wasn't learning anything there and that I literally knew more than the teacher, and more important I had an interest in learning, which she didn't have. So my family and I decided I could move into the town where I had been before, where there were pretty good schools, but I didn't have any money and they didn't have any money. I was 15 then. I arranged to go to a town called Humboldt near Brazil in west Tennessee. An old friend there that I'd met in the Cumberland Presbyterian Church, where my family went to church, had a garage that had been made over for a house servant who was no longer living there.

They let me sleep in their garage and I had a sterno-can heater for cooking. That was my kitchen. I was going to high school and I got odd jobs mowing lawns and things like that. Then finally I got a job working part-time in a grocery store. So from then on I started earning my own living.

Now my parents, who were still living in the country, would come in a wagon and a team of mules from fifteen miles away every week or two to shop, and if they had some potatoes or something on the farm they could share with me, they'd bring that, but that was the best they could do. They were determined that I have a chance to go to school because that was important to them, and I never questioned them. Just never occurred to me not to go to school. It was just one of these things that never came up. The question was, *how* do you go to school? Where do you go to school? I think it's that kind of family background that was very important to my curiosity about learning and interest in getting an education.

I can remember very well that I never felt sorry for myself. I just accepted the fact that those were the conditions and that I was a victim of those conditions, but I never had any feeling of inferiority to other people. I think I got that from my parents too, because even though they were struggling and they were poor, they never accepted the fact that they were inferior to anybody or that anybody was inferior to them. That just wasn't part of our vocabulary. It wasn't part of the thinking. So I didn't have the handicap of feeling sorry for myself or blaming people who were in a better position than I was, because I guess somehow I sensed very early on it was the system's fault and not the people's fault. I never was much into blaming people, even though some people were oppressive, because I figured they were victims of the system just like I was a victim of the system. I don't think I made that kind of analysis as clearly as that, but I know that was my feeling, so I was free from wasting a lot of energy feeling sorry for myself. I stress that because I had an experience that cleared that problem up once and for all when I was going to school at Brazil, out in the country from Humboldt.

I was 13 or 14. And I used to have to ride a bony horse four miles or walk to school. We didn't have a saddle, so I got tired and sore riding that old horse. So I decided I'd rather walk. I walked four miles there and four miles back. But in the meantime I belonged to what was called the 4-H Club. That's an organization of farm young people that at that time was into helping young people learn to farm. One of the things that they promoted was pride in growing the best chickens or the best pumpkin or the best hog, and I had what looked like was going to be a winner of a prize—and I never won any prizes for anything in my life—a hog that I'd grown from a little pig. Somebody had given me the pig and I fed it on the bottle and raised it, and it got to be a fat pig. For the first time in my life, I was looking forward to getting some kind of recognition for something I had done. I thought the 4-H Club would give me a blue ribbon for this pig.

We had to eat the pig because we didn't have any other food. My feeling was that I was being put upon by my family, that I was being taken advantage of. I started feeling very sorry for myself, and I went out behind the barn in the clover field. It was summertime and the moon was shining and I walked out in that clover field and I started crying. I felt so sorry for myself. I just thought I had been mistreated. And I finally just stretched out in the clover, and I was there in the clover sobbing away, and here's the moon and the stars out, everything was silent. Suddenly I thought how ridiculous this is. Nobody knows. The moon can't hear me. The stars can't hear me. The clover can't hear me. No human beings around. Here I am feeling sorry for myself, and nobody knows it. So what's this all about. And right there in the clover field I decided I would never be sorry for myself again, that that was not the way to go. That incident with the pig hurt me, but it didn't bother anybody else. Didn't change anything. So it's absurd. And besides, why should I feel sorry for myself when actually the cause of my sorrow was family survival. No fault of my parents. It was the fault of something else.

When I stopped feeling sorry for myself and I started looking at where the blame was, not in my parents but in the situation that my parents found themselves, there I was beginning to understand that there are nonpersonal sources, which I later identified with an oppressive system. At that time I just knew that they weren't to blame. I knew my dad had hunted everywhere for jobs. He'd been laid off every job he had. He was doing the best he could, and my mother was trying to make do with limited resources. They loved us but they were crippled. They were handicapped by this situation. And from that time on, I never felt sorry for myself. I never felt that it was of any importance. I was just a mighty small unit in this beautiful sky above, in the clover field. My concerns should not dominate my thinking. I think I got a little objectivity at that time.

Now there's times when I was tempted to feel sorry for myself, but I always built on it. I remember when I was in high school I was working, going to school, borrowing other people's books, there was an evening violin concert, which cost a quarter. Well I didn't have a quarter, but I wanted to hear the concert. So I stood outside where I could hear it. It started raining and I tried to get in the front door so I could be in the dry and listen, but my teacher wouldn't let me in because I didn't have a quarter. I can think of periods like that when I was resentful, very resentful. But I wasn't resentful at the teacher who wouldn't let me in. I'd already gotten beyond that stage. I was resentful at the situation that caused this. So I think I kind of liberated myself by that experience in the clover fields, so I could begin to think of other things. Since I didn't have to waste any of my sympathy on myself, I had a lot more sympathy for other people.

PAULO: Myles, could you read?

MYLES: I learned to read even before I went to school because we had books in the family. We didn't have many, but even before we left Savannah where I grew up until the seventh or eighth grade, I'd been a reader. I read so much that I'd borrow books from everybody. We didn't have money to buy books, so I read everybody else's books. I would go house to house and ask them if they had any books I could read. I remember very well when a cousin of mine moved in from the country. He was crippled and his family were quite well-to-do farmers, and they retired and moved. They had a bookcase, a beautiful big glass-covered bookcase with several feet of books and ten or fifteen rows of books. I started looking at those books. I'd never seen so many books together in anybody's house. We didn't have a library in that town, and school didn't have any books, so I asked if I could read these books, and they said, "Well yes." It was a collection of old books that the family had collected, dictionaries and religious books, books on medicine, books on animal husbandry and all, dictionaries, encyclopedias—the whole collection. I said I could keep them in order if I just can go down one shelf and another, and they were amazed that anybody would read books that way.

They didn't know that I had no taste about reading at all. I just read words, and I never had a problem of having any choices to make. It never occurred to me that you picked this book against that book. You just read them all, read any book you could find. I read dictionaries. I read encyclopedias. I read dirty stories, and I read pornography, and I read religious tracts. I read whatever was next on the shelf. And I just read everything, so that's sort of a background on reading. That's why I comment on the fact that the town of Brazil didn't have any books and I didn't have any books and we couldn't afford to buy books and nobody else in that part of the country had any books, so that was a year of not being able to get books.

PAULO: But, Myles, look. As far as you can remember, how

did you relate your childhood experience before going
to school with the knowledge you got, with the experience of the student Myles. You remember?

MYLES: I was always getting in trouble for reading in school.
I was reading things that weren't assigned, and I'd get
criticized for it. I used to put books behind the geography book because it was big, and I'd put the geography
book on the desk. I wasn't smart enough to think the
teacher would keep seeing me studying geography all
the time and nothing else. Finally the teacher walked
around while I was concentrating on my book and came
in behind me. She tapped me on the shoulder and suddenly I realized that she was standing behind me seeing
what was behind the geography book. I can remember exactly what I was reading. It was a series of books
about the boys in India and around the world. It was
a travelogue, sensational stories of adventure. And I
was in India. I wasn't there in that schoolroom. The
teacher actually opposed my reading because you were
supposed to study, and that's supposed to take all your
time, studying these lifeless textbooks that I'd already
read. I'd read through the geography the first day; I
didn't need to study that. I just went through that like I
went through everything else. It was just another book
to read to me. Then I read the Bible twice all the way
through like a book. It's a great book, one of the best
books I ever read. I grew up reading, and that stood me
in good stead a lot of times even when I was in college
later on.

THIRD PARTY: Did your mother actually teach you to read?

MYLES: I don't know how I learned to read. People used

to ask me—when I lived at Savannah and I was borrowing their books—how I learned to read so young,
and I couldn't remember. I couldn't tell anybody how I
learned to read.

PAULO: I read in your text,* which you read in Copenhagen,
a very interesting scene, the precise moment in which
you started recognizing, in a much more deepened way,
the *value* of the books. That is precisely when you went
on more deeply in reading *reality,* drawing from your
experience. The longer ago it is, the more you began
to reflect on the experience and the more you discover
the value of the books.

I think that it's very interesting, because sometimes
we can fall into some mistakes, for example, the mistake
of denying the value of books, the value of reading, or
denying the value of practice. I think we have to understand how books as theory and practice as action must
be constantly dialectically together, that is, as a unity
between practice and theory. I think that this is one
of the most important dimensions of your own life because of what happened many years ago when you went
to school. It was some years later before you started
being challenged. You went to Denmark to see what
happened there, but undoubtedly your experience of
reading, as a boy before going to this Danish school,
and your experience afterward in the school helped

* Myles Horton, "Influences on Highlander Research and Education
Center, New Market, TN, USA," paper presented at a Grundtvig
workshop, Scandinavian Seminar College, Denmark, 1983; published in *Grundtvig's Ideas in North America—Influences and Parallels*
(Copenhagen: Det Danske Selskab [Danish Institute], 1983).

you to know how far school was from the experience of life, your way of trying to understand constantly what you were doing. All these things have to do with the experiences and the theory that we find inside of the practice here [at Highlander].

MYLES: At first, you see, during the period I was telling you about, I didn't connect books with life. I didn't connect books with reality. They were just entertainment, and I was just reading mechanically. That's why I didn't make any distinction between books. I had no taste or discrimination. I was just reading to read. I guess it gave me some facility in reading, but actually I didn't try to read fast, I didn't try to read for understanding. I just tried to read because I didn't have anything else to do. It was later on that I started thinking books had something in them for me. By the time I was in the high school, I was beginning to read to make sense. It was earlier that I just read everything and didn't care what was in it. I was beginning to learn there were things in books that were worth knowing, not just entertainment. I was reading more seriously, more selectively.

I can remember that I enjoyed reading Shakespeare and a lot of the classics. The rest of the students hated them because they just read excerpts and they just read them for exams. At that period I was working and I didn't have any money to buy textbooks. So I was borrowing my classmates' textbooks so I wouldn't have to buy them. That's when I learned to read fast because I had to get the books, read them fast, and get back to them. In return for that, I would slip them answers

to questions on exams. We'd trade. I'd give them the
answers to the questions if they'd loan me their books.

PAULO: But, Myles, I would like to come back to some point
in your reflections about reading and pleasure and the
examination, for example. I also love to read because I
never could separate reading and pleasure; but I'm as
glad, for example, in reading a good novelist as I am
glad in reading Gramsci. You see, for me, starting to
read a text is first a hard task, a difficult task. It's not
easy. Starting is not easy. For me what is fundamental
in the role of the teacher is to help the student to discover that inside of the difficulties there is a moment of
pleasure, of joy. Of course, if I am reading a novel it
is easier for me because I am involved in an aesthetical
event that I don't know how to finish. In some way I also
may be rewriting the beauty I am reading. When I am
reading Gramsci, Vygotsky, or Giroux or when I was
reading your writing this morning, I also am and was
in search of some beauty, which is the knowledge I have
there. That is, I have to grasp in between the words
some knowledge that helps me not exclusively to go on
in the reading and in *understanding* what I'm reading,
but also to understand something beyond the book I
am reading, beyond the text. It is a pleasure. For me
there is a certain sensualism in writing and reading—
and in teaching, in knowing. I cannot separate them.
Knowing for me is not a neutral act, not only from the
political point of view, but from the point of view of my
body, my sensual body. It is full of feelings, of emotions,
of tastes.

23

"Reading has to be a loving event"

PAULO: I learned how to read and to write with my father and my mother under the trees of the backyard of my house. Mango trees. And I used to write in the dirt with a piece of twig. It's very interesting. I knew words with which I started my learning were words of my horizon, of my experience, and not the words of the experience of my parents. They started doing that to me. It's very fantastic because many years later when I was beginning to work in this field as an educator, I repeated what my parents did with me. I remembered during the process that it was like this that I learned how to read and to write.

I did not have, nevertheless, the same richness of experience that Myles had. I did not read as much as he read, for example. I was born some eight years before the big crash—I was born in 1921—and my middle class family suffered a lot of the consequence of that. I had the possibility to experience hunger. And I say I had the *possibility* because I think that that experience was very useful for me. Of course my childhood was not so dramatic. I could eat anyway. Millions of Brazilian children today don't eat, but at least I could eat, something that made it possible for me to survive. I entered the secondary school much older than the average student. I was in the first year of the secondary school when I was 16 years old, and it was too much for the normal students. I remember that I had difficulty understanding. Sometimes I considered myself stupid because I had such difficulty understanding the normal and bureaucratic lessons of my school. I suffered a lot because I thought that I was very stupid. That is, I didn't know it should be better, but I thought that I was stupid, and in thinking that I was, I suffered. In fact I had difficulty understanding for different reasons, not exclusively because I was hungry but mainly due to the very *process* of schooling, the very deficiencies of some of the schools I was in. Since that time, I believed that even though I was not convinced about my capacity of learning, it should be possible to learn. I laughed, too, but I did not love the ways I was being taught. Afterward, in the secondary school, I had good experiences with some teachers who challenged me more than the others. Little by little I came into this kind of discovery.

THIRD PARTY: What were your parents doing and how did that affect their work?

PAULO: My father died very young. He was 52 years old when he died. It's a very strange experience for me to know that I am older than my father. He was a military man but a democratic one, very democratic one. When he retired he could not do anything more, just receive a small amount of money.

My mother was not prepared to work, unless inside of the house. All that my father got normally from his retirement was not enough for us to live on well. In 1934, he died, and I was 13 years old. Then the situation became more difficult. We did not have at that time in Recife (it's my city) public schools at the level of secondary school. My mother had to try to find a secondary school where I could start without paying. She tried a lot. Every day she left the house to search for a school. I was waiting for her, full of hope, but without being sure, and she said nothing, nothing. But one day she arrived, I went to receive her on the train, and she was smiling. She said, "Today I got a school for you." Until today I have a strong feeling of gratitude to the couple—the director, Alvizio Araujo, and his wife, Genove—who gave me the possibility of being here today, talking with Myles. It has to do with being here with Myles now because Araujo made it possible for me to go to school. He was the director of a fantastic secondary school in Recife that was very famous at that time.* I always like to express my gratitude to him.

For me the virtue of gratitude is fundamental to human beings. But of course I don't understand gratitude in order to do what my conscience says to me that I could not do. For example, I never would vote for a reactionary person in order to be grateful. But taking it from the discussion, I would do everything I could for this director and his wife.

When I started studying in this school, I felt so challenged by some of the teachers that in three years I could teach Portuguese language and syntax. The more possibility I had to read the good Brazilian and Portuguese grammars, philogists, linguistics, the more I could discover this question of taste.

I discovered that reading has to be a loving event. I still remember when I was not yet married, being

* Araujo was the director of Osvaldo Cruz School. In 1988 Paulo married Araujo's daughter, Ana Maria Araujo, historian and the author of *Analfabetismo No Brasil*, a history of illiteracy in Brazil (São Paulo: INEP, 1989).

alone in the small house where we used to live—reading, making notes, observations, at two o'clock in the morning. Sometimes my mother used to come in to say to me, "It is too much. You have to sleep." But I had such an almost physical connection with the text. It was this experience that began to teach me how reading is also an act of beauty because it has to do with the reader rewriting the text. It's an aesthetical event.

I was maybe 19 years old. And I always remember that it was a great feeling of happiness. Because of that, I said to Myles that it's no different for me if I am reading poetry or if I am reading Marx. I try to get the beauty in the very act of reading, you see. This is for me something that many times teachers don't try to do.

MYLES: They try to kill off this beauty actually.

PAULO: The students read, as Myles said, because they are *obliged* to read some text, whose relationship with the context they don't grasp.

MYLES: I can remember, when I was in high school, how sad I was that my classmates didn't like to read poems, stories, literature. I enjoyed it so much and they hated it. I thought it was the teachers that did that to them, and I resented that. I could see this system, where teachers were killing off any possibility of students ever enjoying this literature. To them it was something that you had to learn, memorize, and you hated it because you had to do it. And I can remember very clearly how I took my resentment out on the teachers. I didn't at that stage speak out and challenge them or try to organize a campaign against them, but I would read in their classes and ignore them. That was my way of protesting, my way of saying don't interfere with my reading. I have more important things to do than to fool with your silly questions. It was always a contest. I always had problems. The teachers resented my lack of respect for them.

I can remember very well the wife of the superintendent, who could never have gotten a job if she hadn't been his wife. She resented me most of all. In her class, she asked me a lot of questions, so I had to listen. But I refused to stop reading, and she was always trying to trick me into stopping. I'd listen to her questions with one ear all the time because I knew it was a game. I didn't care what question it was, I was going to be ready to answer it at the same time I was reading. This used to make her furious because I could do that. So I carried on this battle with the teachers all through high school. I didn't respect them because I thought they were killing all the creativity. I became very critical of the way things were done. I had no way of expressing this except ignoring them to show what I thought, but I did develop a critical attitude at that time.

There's two things in my life that were very important in terms of where I spent my time, one was school and the other was church. In that little town, many of us were interested in education or religion. That's where people were. That's where the social life was. Part of my life was in a church community, part was in the school community, the other part was in a work community. When I was in high school there were two things that happened in this little Cumberland Presbyterian Church in Humboldt, where I was going to high school. One of them was a missionary who was telling how many souls he had saved in Africa, and I was impressed with that. I thought that was great, saving souls, until he says the ones that I didn't save are going to hell. I said wait a minute. Something's wrong with this kind of thinking. He said if they're told about Christ and they don't accept him, then they go to hell, but if they aren't told, then they don't go to hell because they aren't responsible. So I did a little mental arithmetic (at which I was very poor but good enough for that purpose) and figured out how many people he was damning to hell, how many people he had told that weren't converted and how many people he sent to hell. The more I thought about that, the more incensed I got at this whole procedure, damning these people to hell. The missionary had a discussion period, and all these people were asking theological questions. So I asked him an arithmetic question. I asked, "How many people have you sent to hell? According to your analysis, for every person you've saved, you've sent hundreds to hell. Why, wouldn't it have been better if you'd stayed home, there'd be more people in heaven if you had stayed home?" Well the people were furious!

As a high school kid, I was active in the church. I was head of the youth group at the church at the time and an active church worker, but I was beginning to get very critical. I was willing to speak up because I felt comfortable there, I felt at home and I thought I could do that. Of course I found out after I did that, I wasn't supposed to ask questions or even think about anything like that.

29

Even later on in the same period I spoke out. I was the head of a regional religious youth group, and I was presiding over a meeting. I got up at the introduction and said we've got a lot of work to do because we've got to talk about religion six days a week instead of one day. Most of the people are just concerned about it on Sunday, and we got to take care of the rest of the week. The preacher said, "Now, Myles, that's an insult, you know." I said, "Well working in the store where I work I realize that the people, a lot of them officials in this church, don't live their religion during the week. They lie, they're hypocrites, they steal." He said, "What do you mean?" I said, "In my job I see things that you don't see." I was somebody in the church, but in that store I was a servant. I found out who paid the bills for some black children, who cheated on their bill, who said food was spoiled when it wasn't. These were leading citizens. I was just fed up with this whole hypocrisy, and I was just ready to explode about this Sunday religion. A lot of my learning came out of not books but working in that store. It's interesting that I could feel free to speak out, was able to speak out in the church, whereas I couldn't find a mechanism for speaking out in the high school except by my show of disrespect.

It was at that stage that reading took on a completely different meaning to me because I was beginning to deal with real problems in life. When I'd read, I was informed by that reading. I'd get ideas from the reading, I'd get emboldened by it, especially poetry, and it took a new meaning. I was no longer reading to pass the time away. Oh, I enjoyed reading. I was able to tie books and reading with life. I can remember very well how I began to be much more selective, saying I can't just read this book because it's next on the shelf anymore. I was beginning to make that connection but I was still coming at it from a book point of view.

PAULO: What fascinates me in reading good books is to find the moment in which the book makes it possible for me or helps me to better my understanding of reality, of concreteness. In other words, for me the reading of books is important to the extent that the books give me a certain theoretical instrument with which I can make the reality more clear vis-à-vis myself, you see. This is the relationship that I try to establish between *reading words and reading the world*. I always was interested in understanding, as you were, the reality, which I mean reading reality. But the process of reading reality in which we are enveloped demands, undoubtedly, a certain theoretical understanding of what is *happening* in reality. Reading of books makes sense for me to the extent that books have to do with this reading of reality.

There have been many books during my process of permanent *formação,* or formation. There were many books, and there are still, which made it possible for me to better my understanding of the phenomena. This is for me what we should propose to the students. It has to do with reading the *text* in order to understand the *context*. Because of that, I have to have some information about the context of the author, the person who wrote the book, and I have to establish some relationship between the time and the space of the author, and with my context. I cannot just suggest the students read Gramsci. I feel obliged to say something about the time and the space of Gramsci. I cannot just translate Gramsci into Portuguese because in order to make this translation, it's necessary for me to understand the context in which he wrote and he thought. In reading him, many times I couldn't have said it better myself. And it is for me beautiful.

I come back again to the question of beauty, and also to the question of keeping the problem of beauty. I would like to say something and maybe you agree with me. It has been told us, is it right, that beauty in writing is a question for literature. The scientist is not obliged to grasp the aesthetical moment of language. The more a scientist writes beautifully, the less of a scientist he or she is. For me it is not right. It is a mistake. For me the scientist who is not able to write beautifully minimizes his or her science and falls into an ideological lie, according to which the scientists have to escape from beauty.

Let us say that beauty and simplicity are not virtues to be cultivated exclusively by the *literatos*, but also by scientists. The scientist is not obliged, just because he or she is a scientist, to write ugly. This is why I always insist on saying to my students that writing beautifully does not mean scientific weakness. It is, on the contrary, a kind of duty we have. The writers, no matter if they are scientists or philosophers, have to make understanding easier.

MYLES: That's why poetry is so wonderful. Poetry is more selective in the use of words to create images and feelings, more selective than prose quite often, and certainly more than scientific academic writing.

I was just trying to think, as you were talking, about how what you were saying related to my experiences in reading. As I was saying earlier, the time came when I was beginning to relate what I read to life experiences. The example I used was relating what I had read in the Bible and the Christian principles I had been taught to every day practice—where these principles weren't carried out. I was beginning to see the contradictions between what I had read and what I had come to believe and what I learned experientially. They are altogether different things. At the same time I was beginning to test out in life things I'd read in books and relate them to my own experience. I still enjoy reading poetry, novels, essays, reading about nature and things that don't have any immediate practical connection with the problems I'm dealing with, but that are a source of creative imagination, keeping me from getting too practical. I carried through my life this interest in reading things just for the sheer joy of reading them, which I don't find at all unconnected with what I do. Sometimes I get my best ideas from something that has nothing to do with my work.

That doesn't mean that I didn't get to the stage when I consciously read very selectively things I thought would be helpful in understanding what I was experiencing. For example, later on, when I was trying to figure out what I wanted to do with my life, I very consciously read books like the history of the utopias and the great Russian novels. I read things that I thought I would enjoy reading but at the same time give me some insights into what I was trying to do.

I made a statement about reading once back during the industrial union period when Highlander was involved in labor organizations and labor education. Many groups—the CIO, the Catholic Church, the Communist Party, the Socialist Party—were setting up schools to be part of this wave of interest in labor education. A young priest from Nashville asked me: "What makes Highlander work? What we do doesn't work. Workers won't come to our classes, but people come here." Who are you, he was saying, and what is it that helps you understand how to make this thing work? He asked me what two or three books have influenced me. I said that if I look back and think of the influences that have been most important to me in trying to figure out what to do, they were the Bible, Shelley, and Marx. First was the Bible because it gave me an ethical background. It gave me a sense of the great religious truths and insights, and I was shaped a lot by that in terms of my values. Then I said I became discouraged with the people who were "religious," and I was turned off by their hypocrisy. I was beginning to lose the kind of faith and inspiration that had been helpful as I was growing up, and I was getting very cynical. Earlier on in high school I had been interested in Shelley, but I had not read him very carefully. I reread some of Shelley's poems that I had read in high school. I read *Prometheus Unbound*, where Shelley defies the people's threats and punishment and the bribery. Shelley stands against that. This young poet was standing for social justice and saying that's the important thing. I got very excited and I reread all of Shelley, and that really straightened me out in a way. It gave me a feeling that I wasn't going to give up. I wasn't going to be subverted by what I was seeing. I was going to do what I wanted to do regardless of anything, and the way to do it was not to be afraid of punishment and not to be tempted by rewards. Not to want to be famous, nor get rich, have power, or be afraid of hell or threats and ostracism. It started me on another line of thinking. I started to take more control of my own life and not be influenced so much by what other people thought or said or did. I got to the place where I was terribly concerned about how I could relate my values to society. At that time I said it's not important to be good, it's important to be good for something. But, what was that something I could be good for, and how could I figure out how to be useful in society and make a contribution?

That's when, in reading everything I could find to try to help me, I ran into Marx. When I learned something about Marxism and started reading some of Marx's writings, I realized that here's a way to analyze. This is a way to look at society, Paulo. I wasn't overly impressed with some of Marx's predictions or some of the conclusions he reached, but I was terrifically impressed by the way of analyzing, the way of looking at society. And I was also very much impressed by his devotion to the poor and the fact that he was trying to work out a way to do exactly what I was trying to do, help the poor, the masses of the people. I had that kind of identity with him. That was the third influence. So when I told this priest about these three books he said: "That's not helpful at all! That's just more confusing than ever!" The Bible, Shelley, Marx. Those books played a very important role at certain points in my life.

PAULO: Yes. I remember, for example, how much I was helped by reading Frantz Fanon. That is great writing. When I read Fanon I was in exile in Chile. A young man who was in Santiago on a political task gave me the book, *The Wretched of the Earth*. I was writing *Pedagogy of the Oppressed*, and the book was almost finished when I read Fanon. I had to rewrite the book in order to begin to quote Fanon. You see, this is a beautiful example that I was influenced by Fanon without knowing it. I had different cases like this, in which I felt conditioned, "influenced," without knowing. Fanon was one. Albert Memmi who wrote a fantastic book, *The Colonizer and the Colonized*, was the second. The third one who "influenced" me without knowing it was the famous Russian psychologist Lev Vygotsky, who wrote a beautiful, fantastic book, *Thought and Language*. When I read him for the first time, I became frightened and happy because of the things I was reading. The other influence is Gramsci. Then when I meet some books—I say "meet" because some books are like persons—when I meet some books, I remake my practice theoretically. I become better able to understand the theory inside of my action.

One of the important tasks we should have as teachers should be not to have the experience on behalf of the students. We cannot do that. They have to have their experience. But maybe we should put to the students at least two times in a semester about how we study. How we do. I used to do that with the students. I used to read chapters of books with the students in graduate courses because many times the students don't know yet what reading means. You must give testimony to the students about what it means to read a text. I remember that one day a young student came to me in one of these courses in which I read with the students, and she said to me: "Paulo, the first time I read the *Pedagogy of the Oppressed* I felt bad. I did not like the book. I thought that the book was very, very difficult for me even to understand. Now I discover that I did not know how to read, and I am learning what it means to read."

I think that we should talk with the students about all the implications of writing and reading. We should make clear to them that it is irresponsible to suggest that reading is something easy. It is also bad not to make clear that reading is a kind of research. In this way, studying means finding something, and the act of finding brings with it a certain taste, a certain moment of happiness that is creation and re-creation. No, it's not easy, but it is good to be done. You see, we should challenge students to get this creative moment and never accept their minds becoming bureaucratized, something that has to read between 10 and 11 a.m. and write between 2 and 3 p.m. No, it's not like this! It's like making love—that cannot be determined for Wednesdays and Saturdays. Nothing scheduled about that!

I am sure that one of the most tragic illnesses of our societies is the bureaucratization of the mind. If you go beyond the previously established patterns, considered as inevitable ones, you lose credibility. In fact, however, there is no creativity without *ruptura,* without a break from the old, without conflict in which you have to make a decision. I would say there is no human existence without *ruptura.*

"I couldn't use all this book learning"

MYLES: Thinking back to when I was in college and I still was learning most of the things from books: The college I went to was a little Presbyterian college here in Tennessee. It had a good traditional library. I was majoring in English Literature, but I was also interested in history. I took a course in the French Revolution in which the teacher lectured from a book and then gave an examination on what happened during a certain period. Well, I didn't think so much of the textbook, and I didn't accept the authors' analysis. So I read some other books about the French Revolution, and I formulated my own idea. I was trying to learn while I was reading, seriously trying to understand what went on. So when the professor asked his question, I answered it from another book, a book that he'd never read. So he gave me a failed grade because I'd given the wrong answer. He said I should have paid attention. I said I remembered what he had said, but I just didn't agree with it. He said: "You know you're a student here. You're not supposed to make judgments. You're supposed to listen to me, and when you take an exam, it's on what I taught you." Well I realized that he didn't know anything else and he was so indignant with me because I knew more than he did about that question. That was quite obvious to me. I thought if that's the way this course is going to be, I'm not going to spend my time here, so I just walked out of the class. I didn't think anything about it.

I did that with several teachers along the way, and it never occurred to me to give it any thought. After Highlander was started, I was in a meeting in Nashville, and this same professor comes to the meeting. He said: "I want to introduce myself. I want to pay tribute to Myles Horton because he changed my life." I looked at this guy—my God, what's he going to say? He told that story I told you. He said: "I was furious, but I couldn't get it out of my mind, and the more I thought about it the more I realized what he was saying was true. It's after that year I quit teaching because I knew I wasn't fit to teach. I just wanted to come and say publicly that he was right and I was wrong." That was a tremendous thing for a person to say. He was willing to publicly say that here I was a student who was right and he the professor was wrong.

The one professor that I learned something constructive from was a young sociology professor from the University of Chicago. I was doing a paper on the cooperative started for tobacco growers in Kentucky. I was doing a lot of reading and research and getting all kinds of documentation. I thought I'd done a very good paper because it had all the facts in it and a good analysis. I was expecting to get a good straight A on that, and I got it back with about a B− and a note saying "well-documented, but it isn't who said it but whether it is true." That was a real shocker to me. That was really the beginning of my understanding something. I was getting to be kind of an authority because I thought that was what you were supposed to do. He said, "No, is it true? You decide whether it's true or not." That started me on a whole new course of thinking, so all of my college wasn't wasted. I educated one professor and I learned from another.

THIRD PARTY: You've both talked about learning from reading, and for both of you reading has to be connected to experience. Where did you start learning about learning from experience?

MYLES: I didn't know even when we started Highlander that I had learned some things. I learned from experience and reading (although I had more reading than I had experience). I would analyze experiences I had and try to learn from those experiences, try to figure out what they meant, but not in any kind of systematic way. What I finally decided, after three or four years of reading and studying and trying to figure this thing out, was that the way to do something was to start doing it and learn from it. That's when I first understood that you don't have to look for a model, you don't get the answers from a book. You look for a *process* through which you can learn, read and learn. I was conscious at that time—slowly became conscious because I had all this academic background, you see—that the way you really learn is to start something and learn as you go along. You don't have to know it in advance because if you know it in advance you kill it by clamping this down on the people you're dealing with. Then you can't learn from the situation, can't learn from the people. I understood that. I wrote in this little piece I did in Denmark that we have to *unlearn*. I was at Highlander with a bunch of other people—Jim Dombrowski, John Thompson, very smart academicians—trying to use what we had learned from books. We knew we had to start, but we also didn't know that we couldn't use all that learning. So it wasn't until Highlander started— and we were told in no uncertain terms by the actions of the people we were dealing with that we didn't know what we were talking about—that I first really seriously understood that I couldn't use all this book learning. This [book learning] was such a rich experience to me that I thought it would be valuable to other people, and I didn't understand that I had gotten away from *how* people really learned, except in academic circles.

Two things happened in the early years of Highlander that are very important. We all agreed we had to start learning from the people we were working with, and that we had to learn from each other. We all learned together, and when I talk about what I learned then, a lot of it I learned from other staff members. I learned a tremendous lot from Zilphia,* my wife, who brought in a whole new cultural background, drama and dance and music, oral history, storytelling—all kinds of things that I'd grown up knowing but just hadn't thought of as being related to learning. So a lot of the learning

---

* Zilphia Mae Johnson was born in Paris, Arkansas. She met Myles when she attended a two-month residential session at Highlander in January of 1935. They were married in March 1935. Zilphia died in 1956.

I got came from staff together trying to learn from the people. And that was the beginning of what really became Highlander. That was how the transition was made.

THIRD PARTY: Did you consciously reflect and study together?

MYLES: We talked. We had meetings. We discussed what the hell we were learning. We laughed! Three of us had been in Union Theological Seminary together, so you know we had some academic background. We all studied with Reinhold Niebuhr. We were Depression-era products. We were in that kind of radical period in American history where people were beginning to question the system, where people were beginning to think. We'd been stimulated by the explosive sort of thinking of Niebuhr and people like him, who kind of blew your mind. Dietrich Bonhoeffer was there at Union as a student when I was. There were other students you'd know about today, but of course when we were there nobody knew anything about any of us.

At Highlander, we were learning together. I think we really kind of had our comeuppance in a way. We thought we had a lot of answers to things, and we suddenly realized that we didn't know much. So here we were, all struggling to learn together at Highlander. We had the same kind of a problem. That's really the beginning. It took something like that for us to move over and start with experience, letting book knowledge throw whatever light it could on that. We became less important in the process than the people we were working with. Before we had that insight, we thought at least we were equal with the people we were dealing with. But we didn't know that we had to keep out of the act. Our job was to get *them* to act. Then we reacted to that action and used whatever we could bring to bear on it. So there was a whole inversion.

THIRD PARTY: You said before that you felt at that time you all had the answers to the questions that you thought the people ought to have.

MYLES: That's right.

THIRD PARTY: When and how did you learn that the questions that you had, that you thought they ought to have, weren't the ones they had?

MYLES: When they weren't paying any attention to us. When we saw that we weren't talking about their needs. We were going to bring democracy to the people, I mean bring it to them like a missionary and dump it on them whether they liked it or not. We thought we were going to make them world citizens. All of us had traveled, we'd been around, abroad, and we'd read all this stuff, and we were going to bring all this enlightenment to the people. We knew how to do it—organize unions and cooperatives and political action and have educational programs. We knew about how to do those things. Some of us had done some of it before. All of us had some experience before. We were further along in our political thinking than most people in the United States at that time. So we thought we were pretty good, but the people didn't pay any attention to anything we were doing. Nothing we were doing they reacted to. We couldn't

43

even talk a language they understood. A lot of their language was nonverbal. We were verbal. We were all certified as verbal, but we couldn't communicate!

THIRD PARTY: What was it that happened in your lives that allowed each of you to come to the understanding that you have, the sort of insight and understanding that you have about people and their knowledge and their experiences and the role that plays in education and working for political change.

MYLES: I think many people who are interested in human values—particularly people who are socialized here in the South through their religious background—are motivated to try to find some way to be useful and serve. This can be a self-serving individualism. I think the problem is that most people don't allow themselves to experiment with ideas, because they assume that they have to fit into the system. They say how can I live out these things I believe in within the capitalist system, within the subsystem of capitalism, the microcosm of capitalism, the school system and within the confines of respectability, acceptance. Consequently, they don't allow themselves to think of any other way of doing things. I don't think there's anything unique in having the kind of ideas that we have. That's kind of nickel-a-bushel stuff, I think. I just think most people can't think outside the socially approved way of doing things and consequently don't open up their minds to making any kind of discoveries. I think you have to think outside the conventional frameworks.

I started thinking outside the conventional frameworks fairly early. We talked about that a little bit already. I was challenging the system, challenging the conventionalities and beginning to ask questions and beginning to not have any respect for the schooling system fairly early, so I suppose I was not too confined trying to fit into the system. My mind could follow its own discoveries to a greater extent than some other people who are less liberated from that kind of constraint.

But the reason I'm making this analysis is because I was fitting into that framework to begin with, and I thought you had to do that. It just didn't occur to me that there's any way you could work outside of the approved ways of working, what you got paid to do. You've got to have somebody to hire you, and you had to think of what you had to do to get hired, in other words how you're going to accept the whole capitalist framework of having to work for somebody so they can make money out of your labor. Then you've got to think about providing profits for them or they wouldn't have any incentive to keep you. Or if you're going to work for the government or for some religious organization or something like a labor organization, then you've got to satisfy *their* demands. You have to think in terms of, "How can I choose among one of these things that I like to do knowing full well that I'll have to do what they tell me to do?" That I didn't question for a while, and I was on the borderline of raising those questions in my mind, but I hadn't quite got around to thinking other than individualistically. In college I was still thinking you had to fit into those systems and frameworks.

One of the first experiences I had that touches on

this, as far as I can remember, is this: I was active in college and I was trying to work out a program for the Student YMCA. I was president of the Student YMCA, and we were trying to deal with discrimination on a world basis as well as a local basis—you know the whole business of fear in spirit, of oppression, and so on. There were a couple of young Jewish students from New Jersey that I was rooming with (we had a house), and a couple of other people, none of whom were interested in this particular topic. I had exhausted all of my resources, all the things I could think of. I couldn't think of anything that wouldn't be repetitious or boring. One of these friends asked me what I was thinking about, what was on my mind, and I just told them what my problem was. Well, within five minutes they had suggested a half dozen things I'd never thought of, because they were coming in from a fresh point of view. They just tried to help me solve a problem, and I was struck with that because it never occurred to me that I could get help from people, except from the people who were involved in exactly the same thing I was involved in. That was a very enlightening experience, and I very consciously noted that down as a way to get things done. I started using that much more widely when I'd run up against a problem. When I couldn't think of a good way to do something, I would involve the first person I saw in a conversation about it or get some people to talking about it because I found I could learn things from other people that up to that time I thought I had to work out for myself. I didn't make much of it at the time, but it started a new kind of practice for me, an appreciation of having the group make a contribution instead of me as an individual. And instead of demoted I got elevated to another level. Instead of feeling less confident I felt more confident, and it didn't make me feel like I was dependent. It made me feel more independent, because it was a constructive experience. Well that was one event that led me to thinking outside conventional frameworks.

The next one was when I was working in the Cumberland mountains for the Presbyterian Sunday School Board. At first, my job was to start and run the daily vacation Bible schools in connection with mountain churches. After the first year, I had a little staff of people who worked with other students. I was beginning to lose interest in just doing that kind of thing because that was getting kind of boring. I didn't see it had much of a potential for going very far. But I liked to work in the mountains and I needed the money and I wanted to get the experience, so I got to the place where I could get my staff to run the Bible schools. They liked it. They were like I was in the first year, and they didn't mind doing it. So I was free to do other things. I was getting paid to do one thing, and I was doing other things.

One of the things I was trying to do was to work with adults, not with children. I was more interested in adult education than childhood education. I was working with a county farm agent who was starting cooperatives. I learned a lot—some positive, some negative things—about cooperatives in that first experience with him.

47

One time we had a little daily vacation Bible school out in the country from Ozone, Tennessee. There's a waterfall at Ozone up in the Cumberland mountains, and it's a beautiful rugged mountain area. I thought I'd try a little experiment, so I had the children take an announcement back home saying that all the parents, the adults, were invited to a special meeting. I didn't tell them what it was about because I didn't think they'd come if they knew what it was about. So we had a number of people come from several miles around; some walked, some rode horses. I don't think there was one car in that area at that time. And what I did was to start off, kind of like your base community group people, by talking about the Bible and talking about the state teaching Bible school, because that's what they had come for. I took about two minutes on that, and then I said: "You know, I know some of the problems here. I know some of you people are working in mines. Some of you people are trying to make a living on farms. Some of you people are going off and working in textile mills. Some of you are back home, suffering from what happened to you in the mines and in the textile mills." At that time people didn't know about black lung or brown lung. Doctors just said that textile mills and coal mines were healthy, good for you, and that these people had tuberculosis. But I said, "It's getting pretty serious, pretty desperate. Let's talk about some of these problems that we have." So immediately they thought I was going to give them the solutions to their problems.

They started talking about them, and I was hard put, see, because I hadn't thought this thing out. This was very elementary and I tried the best I could to answer questions from what little I knew. I knew more than they did about a lot of these things, because they might know about the specific situation but they didn't link it up with other situations, with general situations. So I was able to help them a little bit, putting it in some kind of perspective. But that soon ran out; that soon was exhausted in terms of dealing with their problems, and I had to tell them that I didn't know these answers. I suggested that we could get this county agent, and a health person, and maybe somebody connected with the unions, who could bring in resources. But they were not satisfied with something in the future, and more in desperation than anything else, I remembered my college experience about turning to other people and getting ideas from others. So I said: "Well let's talk about what you've done, maybe what you know will help somebody else and what they've done to help you. Let's talk about what you know. You know this better than anybody else. You don't have any answers, but you know the problems."

That was the beginning of this understanding that there's knowledge there that they didn't recognize. I didn't have any terminology for this or any concepts for this but that's what it was, you see. And to my surprise and to their surprise—we were all equally surprised because we were all equally naive about this—before the evening was over people began to feel that from their peers they were beginning to get a lot of answers.

So that was my second learning experience, but I still didn't know what I knew. Just like they didn't know what they knew, I didn't know what I knew. But I kept talking about it and thinking about it, and that experience was kind of tucked away, not right up front. It was there in my psych, always kind of nagging at me, but I couldn't quite get at it. The reason I couldn't get at it was because I was trying to fit things into the *traditional* way of doing things. I couldn't see how this was part of anything that I knew anything about and I couldn't quite bring myself to think there were ways of doing things outside the system. I was so socialized to accept that, that I was still limited by that. It didn't really ring a bell very loud. The bell was ringing but was very low, and when it would start ringing I'd kind of cover it up so I wouldn't have to listen to it, because I didn't understand it.

Well, that was the beginning of that kind of experience, but Ozone to me was more than just that experience. After I had held adult meetings for a couple of weeks, the word spread that there were people coming from miles around, coming every night, and that was a phenomenon they weren't used to. There was a lady who owned a big house in Ozone who was getting ready to retire, and she found out about my meetings and invited me to dinner at her house. She wanted to know what I was doing in stirring up all this discussion, and some of it was negative. And she said she'd like for me to come there and live and do this kind of a program. Well, that was completely beyond anything I could think of at that time, you know. I was still going to school. I had one more year in college, and I knew I wasn't ready to settle down. So I thanked her and said, maybe later on, maybe after a few years. Right then I didn't want to do that because I really didn't feel I had any grasp of anything. I used that concept of Ozone not because of the experience I had with the people but because it was a *place* and I need to think in terms of place, like High-lander to me is a place. Ozone was a place. John's Island, where the Citizenship School started, was a place. My mind's just more comfortable dealing with something I could see. So from then on, any time I'd have an idea that I thought was germane with what I wanted to do, I would put it down on notes, *Ozone* and I used "O," a circle. But the circle was Ozone and the circle was these people; it kind of combined everything. So at Union Theological Seminary, my notes there had Ozone, you know, "O." So Ozone stayed in my mind.

Well that's pretty much the background of my chang-ing ideas. From then on I was trying to figure out intel-lectually, you see, what to do. I spent one year in college, one year working out of college, about three more years in school and in Denmark trying to figure this thing out, and what I was doing was still looking for a model. I was still looking somewhere else outside of my own experi-ence for something, some solution to this problem I had of what I was going to do with my life and how I was going to work. I was still stuck in that business of trying to fit it in, so I did two kinds of things. One, I went back into history because I thought maybe something I could learn would throw light on my situation, and in the process of doing that I got interested in the uto-pian communities. Here's some people who struggled with this same problem. I read all the books I could on

utopias. I thought maybe that's the answer, these uto-
pian colonies, these communes, getting away from life,
and kind of separating yourself and living your own
life. I was attracted to it but I was very skeptical from
the very beginning. It seemed to be too precious, too
"getting away" from things. I ended up visiting all the
remains of communes in the United States—Oneida,
Amana, New Harmony in Ohio. Here in Tennessee we
had Rugby, where Thomas Hughes started a Christian
socialist commune, which is now a tourist place. (They
don't tell what it really was.) I ended up concluding
that they were just like I had already concluded—that
a person shouldn't live within himself. I thought that
a group that isolated itself from society shouldn't live
within themselves. That became a center. Life had to go
out, not turn in. And I discarded utopian communities.

Then I started trying to explore other possibilities,
including learning about education in other countries.
And I finally ended up even going to Denmark to see
what the folk schools were like because I was impressed
with what they had accomplished. I read everything on
the folk schools in the University of Chicago library.

THIRD PARTY: Myles, when you say you were still looking
for a model, at what point did you decide that you were
going to do a school?

MYLES: I knew I was going to do something in adult education in the mountains all along, but I didn't know what
form it would take, how to go about it.

THIRD PARTY: So you at this point still weren't thinking
about a school.

MYLES: I was thinking, how do you go about doing an educational job in the mountains. There was nothing in adult education in this country that threw any light on it. I had known Lindeman* and I knew other people who were interested in adult education, but I couldn't relate them back to Ozone. They just didn't seem to fit. I was trying to find something that would fit, something that would be relevant. I wasn't looking for a technique or a method. I wasn't, and you know I still am not. That's not what I've ever been interested in. I was looking for a *process* of how to relate to the people. Finally lightening struck. Finally, it just became very clear that I would never find what I was looking for. I was trying the wrong approach. The thing to do was just find a place, move in and start, and let it grow. It took me, let's see, about six years from the time I got interested. I was a slow learner to find out that I didn't need to know; I just needed to have a vision and that I *shouldn't* know. You should let the situation develop. And of course you've got to use anything that you've learned in the process. Not that all this is wasted, but you have to clear your mind and start over because you can never get going without starting. I was trying to be too rational about it and trying to figure it out in advance.

One reason for this I've already mentioned is constraints of convention. The other reason is I've never felt comfortable experimenting with people, and I think you have a responsibility to go as far as you can in

*   Eduard Lindeman (1885–1953) was a professor of social philosophy, Colombia University School of Social Work. He is best known for his book *The Meaning of Adult Education* (New York: New Republic, 1926).

your head before you go out and just play around with people. So that was part of my problem. I think you do a lot of damage as well as a lot of good. The reason I was aware of that was that here in the mountains we had had missionaries of all kinds—religious missionaries, economic missionaries, government missionaries, political missionaries—all coming down to save the people of Appalachia. I thought a lot of those programs had been detrimental, and I resented the exploitation of people by somebody, particularly from the outside, who came in with an idea they thought was good for people. I didn't want to be another missionary coming in with outside ideas and imposing them on people; that was part of my reservation that I was struggling with.

As I say I was a slow learner. It took me a long time to get comfortable with being free to respond to people. Even having gone through that stage and talked about it and discussed it with my fellow students and with some of the teachers, with many other people, we still got off on the wrong foot when we did it. We still made the mistake of imposing with the best of intentions because that's all we knew. We came out of this academic background and we were still within this orbit of conventionality in education. We said, we're going to let the thing grow, and yet we come in and we say well, the only thing to do is to do education like education is done. We still haven't gotten beyond that stage. But the thing that made Highlander work is that we had a *commitment*. All of us had a commitment to make it work in terms of the people's interest, not in terms of ours. We didn't have any trouble saying the answers we have are for problems people don't have. They've got other problems and we don't have any answers. We didn't have any trouble dealing with that because we were intellectually prepared and emotionally prepared. We had to do some fast shifting around though, because we still hadn't learned how to respond to people, but we were committed to doing it. Once that commitment is made, then you do it. You do whatever it takes. We had to laugh at ourselves for thinking that we could figure out in advance what to do.

That's the whole background, I think, as far as I can see, on what my thinking was that went into this idea of Highlander. It's rather interesting that here we are within seventy-five miles of Ozone, over sixty years later from the time I was there, with the idea that really took form there: people learning from each other. You don't need to know the answer. You can help people get the answers. You have to know something; they know something. You have to respect their knowledge, which they don't respect, and help them to respect their knowledge. These seeds were planted there.

"I always am in the beginning, as you"

MYLES: I'd be interested to know how this sounds to you, Paulo, in terms of what actually took place. Now I know what I *think* took place, but I'd like to know what your reaction is to this. Is this just a construct I'm making of the past, looking back, or is there some reality to it? Am I imagining things or rewriting things?

PAULO: No, I felt very very well listening to you telling us this story. I would like to say something also about my beginnings—in which I still am, because I *always* am in the beginning, as you.

I am convinced that in order for us to create something, we need to start creating. We cannot wait to create tomorrow, but we have to start creating. I am sure that in trying to create something inside of history we have to begin to have some dreams. If you don't have any kind of dream I am sure that it's impossible to create something. The dreams push me in order to make them real, concrete, and the dreams, of course, also are surrounded by values of other dreams. We never finish having dreams. As you said earlier, in a very beautiful language, that you think about climbing the mountain, but suddenly you climb the mountain and discover that there is another one whose profile you could not yet see. Then, without rejecting the first dream, you discover that the first dream, which was the mountain, implies or demands that your dream be expanded into new dreams or visions. In the last analysis, this is the same dream, with different moments. This happened also to me, and it happens with everyone. For example, one of my first dreams, when I was a child, was to teach. I remember until today how I talked to myself about becoming a teacher, and I was still in a primary school.

Thinking back, among other reasons it might have been the difficulties we had in order to eat, for example, but I was already thinking to teach sometime. If you asked me to teach *what,* I did not know at that time, but I thought I had a certain kind of a love for teaching. Today when I think about that, it becomes clear to

56

me. In the last analysis, what I was loving was *knowing*. For me it's impossible to understand teaching without learning, and both without knowing. In the process of teaching, there is the act of *knowing* on the part of the teacher. The teacher has to know the content that he teaches. Then in order for him or for her to teach, he or she has first of all to know and, simultaneously with teaching, to *continue* to know why the student, in being invited to learn what the teacher teaches, *really* learns when the student becomes able to know the content that was taught. It's impossible to escape from knowing that what is important is to know what it *really* means to know. It's impossible to escape from that. Then, in the last analysis, when I had the dream to teach some-day, it was, I am sure, my curiosity, my uneasiness, my questions about the world, about my life, about the dif-ficulties we had, that I wanted to know. Because of that, I used to ask questions even to myself.

There is another very important question aside in my life that has to do with my task as an educator. In my childhood I had *companheiros* who came from dif-ferent social classes. I had *companheiros* from the same position of class that I had. Even today I speak about me and my brother, for example, like "connective" chil-dren, using the magical expression of the conjunction. I was a kind of conjunction, making the relationship between the two classes. And we played soccer together in the street in which we lived. I visited it some months ago, the same street where I played soccer a long, long time ago when I was 9 or 10 years old. I remembered how much it shocked me to be hungry, even though

57

I had something to eat. But I knew *companheiros* who almost did not eat, and they were happy like me in the football game, but they used to tell me in our conversations that they were hungry. And one of the questions I used to ask myself was this one—it was a naive question but an appropriate question for a child like I was—I asked constantly myself why, why is it possible that some children eat and some other ones don't?

It was too much for me to understand that, but when I think of that, I once again see how much I liked to know, to think, to ask questions, to imagine, to realize, and how much I see I've begun in some ways to build the dream I still have. That is, I've begun to dream with a different society. Of course, at that time I could not even put some lines in the drawing of the society, but I remember that at that time in a very concrete way—like the children are concrete—I thought about the society in which Pedro, Carlos, Dourado, and Dino (these were friends) could eat, could study, could live free. I could not imagine at that time what would cause the creation of such a society, but it was my dream.

I was, in fact, beginning to have a vision of a different kind of life, of a different kind of society—a society less unjust, much more humanized. When I was 19 years old, 20 years old, I began to teach. First of all I started teaching privately because in doing that I could help the family, you know. I could help my mother concerning the budget of the family. Then I began to give private classes of syntax and Portuguese language. I still have the taste of having given the first class. It is something that took my body with emotion, a feeling of happiness. I almost cried out in the street after I gave the first class. I taught two or three young people who needed to know something concerning the process of their working activity. When I started I never stopped. I began to teach more and more. People began looking for me, asking me to teach them, and of course I began to buy some important books about grammar by Brazilian and Portuguese grammarians. Afterward, I went beyond grammar and began to study philosophy of language, sociology of language, some books of linguistics.

Suddenly I could teach Portuguese in the same secondary school I spoke about earlier, whose Director Araujo made it possible for me to study when my mother asked him for a place for her son. He invited me to teach. I will never forget that in the third day of teaching in this very famous secondary school, suddenly the director opened the door, came in the room, got his chair, and stayed there in order to listen to my speech class and observe how I worked. It was a beautiful moment of my life. The director was there—silent, serious, without aggression but with his authority of his position and with the authority of his competence. I knew that it was a challenge. I was sure that I could answer the challenge of his presence because I knew the issues I was teaching. Maybe at that time I began to become convinced of this obvious thing. A teacher has to teach, but in order to teach he has to know what he or she teaches. Maybe I learned that so clearly at that moment, many years before today.

When I finished the class the director smiled and

said to me, "Please come to my office." I went with security, do you see? I knew that he could not say, you are bad. I was sure about that. I went with confidence and he said to me: "Paulo, congratulations. You are a very good teacher. You give a beautiful class. But I have to ask you to lower the level of your teaching because I am afraid that some very young students could not understand well. Next time please ask them to feel free to tell you whether they need some explanation."

So I said, "Oh, thank you very much."

He said, "Go ahead, you are very good."

This confirmed something that I already knew, that I was right, that I was becoming competent, and it taught me to be serious. It is necessary, however, to point out that in order for teachers to improve their competency, they need to be respected and they need good salaries. I understand that in many situations in Latin America the teachers cannot teach seriously because they receive such a low salary. Teachers cannot rest because they have to work too much, and they are not able to read when they get to a level of exhaustion. It's impossible. Because of that, I think that the teachers should fight. I am sure that the duty and right of the teachers, because they have to be serious teachers, is to organize themselves in order to fight against discrimination and low wages from many kinds of governments. The only way teachers have to demonstrate to the students that they are serious sometimes is to fight—to fight in order to get a better salary and then to begin to become more competent.

But let's come back to my story. Teaching secondary

school was then an adventure. It was a beautiful thing for me. At some point, I began to discover that one of the main reasons why the students could learn with me and liked my class was that I respected them, no matter their age (very young). I respected them and I respected their mistakes, their errors, and their knowledge. They knew something before coming to the school, and it was important for me in teaching syntax of Portuguese language to know what they knew, because they came to the school with a linguistic competency. We don't teach any language to anyone. Children become competent in a language. After that we can teach the grammar. But *language* we experience, we create. So I respected the students very much.

I also discovered another thing that was very important to me afterward, that I had authority but I was not authoritarian. I remember that not even one of the students ever left the classroom without telling me or asking me in a very respectful, polite way every time. I began to understand at a very young age that on one hand the teacher as a teacher is not the student. The student as the student is not the teacher. I began to perceive that they are different but not necessarily antagonistic. The difference is precisely that the teacher has to teach, to experience, to *demonstrate* authority and the student has to experience freedom in relation to the teacher's authority. I began to see that the authority of the teacher is absolutely necessary for the development of the freedom of the students, but if the authority of the teacher goes beyond the limits authority has to have in relation to the students' freedom, then we no longer have authority. We no longer have a freedom. We have *authoritarianism*. I began to learn these things when I was very young teaching Portuguese language.

After teaching Portuguese language for five or six years, Elza and I met each other. We got married and we have five children and eight grandchildren today. Unfortunately I no longer have Elza. Elza is no longer here in the world. My friends say that she is here. I accept their kindness, but she is not. It's different. Elza exercised a fantastic influence on me, and I would say that she is one of the demarcations in my life. I should say "before Elza," "after Elza," because she was a fantastic educator, very young but very, very good, full of notions and feeling and knowledge of what she was doing. In a preschool, also in the primary school, she was very good in literacy for children. I think for that reason that Elza was better than I. Of course, I think that she was a great educator. In meeting Elza and loving Elza and getting married to Elza, her influence made me much more conscious of what I was doing.

I discovered, because of Elza, that what I was doing in teaching Portuguese was something more than teaching, it was precisely *education*. I don't want to separate teaching from education. That does not make sense. What I want to say is that objectively when I was teaching Portuguese language I was educating. But I did not know it, and it was Elza who *enlightened* me concerning that. Suddenly I began to put together old dreams and to recognize the links among them. It became very clear to me that I had a taste for asking questions, for knowing, for teaching, and I was sure that I was an educator or that I would have to become an educator. This was Elza's first great influence on me because Elza, in fact, exercised an extraordinary influence on me from the existential point of view and from the intellectual point of view. She was an "artist" whose respect for me shaped who I am. In respecting me, she developed many aspects of my profile. Because of that, without Elza possibly I would not be here speaking about this— possibly, but I am not quite sure. It's possible that I would not be here now if it was not for the love for life she had. The love for me, for the kids, for the people, for the students. Her courage of creating things never stopped. It's important. I would like to say that I am not a widower full of nostalgia. I am analyzing some moments in the process of my development, and because of that I think about her influence and her suggestions.

I stopped teaching syntax, and I went to work in 1946 in a new organization that was created in Recife. There I began to get in touch again with workers. Working there in the sector of education, I began to learn lots of things like Myles learned when he began to get contact with workers. He said something that I also will say, more or less in the same way. As a young academic, my conviction was that we had knowledge, we had good knowledge, and the people did not have this.

Subjectively I was not reactionary because I was becoming engaged more and more in favor of the interests of the working class. One other point, related to this one, in which I was mistaken and influenced by the elitist and authoritarian ideology, has to do with the method I used to teach workers. That is, I went to the people and I spoke *to* them without ever speaking *with* them. Look, I am convinced that a progressive educator cannot speak exclusively *with* the people. He or she has also to speak, from time to time, *to* the people. It has to do with the directiveness of education, and directiveness does not mean necessarily authoritarianism or manipulation. Education has the directivity because education has objectives, you see. Education is not neutral, and because of that it has directiveness. I learned like Myles, no? He said some beautiful things. He said, more or less, it took time. Yes, it took time. One of the things that men like us, like lots of other people we know in the world—one of the things that we can do in order to help the younger generation is to tell them our stories and to speak about—

MYLES: How long it takes.

PAULO: How long it takes. Maybe they will shorten their time to learn.

MYLES: One thing about learning is that you have to enjoy it. You said to me in Los Angeles that you wanted to become as a little child like I was. Picasso says it takes a long time to grow young, and I say it takes even longer to become as a little child. So that's the height we are striving for.

PAULO: And Myles, the more we become able to become a child again, to keep ourselves childlike, the more we can understand that because we love the world and we are open to understanding, to comprehension, that when we kill the child in us, we are no longer. Because of that, in Los Angeles my daughter Magdalena said about Myles, "He's a baby!"

MYLES: I fell in love with her right there.

PAULO: Yes. Coming back to my question, it took time for me to learn that the people with whom I was working already had lots of knowledge. The question for me was exclusively to understand what were their levels of knowledge and *how* did they know. I could not understand. Once again Elza was my educator. I remember that she used to come with me every night when I had meetings with workers, inside of Recife or out of Recife. Once a month in each place we had educational programs with teachers and parents. It was a beautiful experience. I learned how to *discuss* with the people. I learned how to respect their knowledge, their beliefs, their fears, their hopes, their expectations, their language. It took time and many meetings.

After one program, Elza and I were coming back home and Elza said to me, with a delicate understanding, "Look, Paulo, it does not work like this." And I asked her: "What did I do? I spoke serious about serious things." She said: "Yes, of course. All you said is right, but did you ask them whether they were interested in listening to you speak about that? You give the answers *and* the questions." You see then? (Look, I would like to make very clear that when I speak about Elza it is not from nostalgia. It's a question of making justice.) And I said, "But Elza." She said: "No, Paulo. You have to change. You cannot grasp the interest of the people while speaking with this language you spoke. It is the language you have to speak at university but not here."

Of course it took time, like Myles said. Even though I had an assistant, Elza, helping me, it took time, but it was through committing these mistakes that I finally learned nevermore to forget that we cannot do anything if we don't respect the people. We cannot educate if we don't start—and I said *start* and not *stay*—from the levels in which the people perceive themselves, their relationships with the others and with reality, because this is precisely what makes their knowledge. In order for one to know, it's just necessary to be alive, then people know. The question is to know what they know and how they know, to learn how to teach them things which they don't know and they want to know. The question is to know whether my knowledge is necessary, because sometimes it is not necessary. Sometimes it is necessary but the need is not yet perceived by the people. Then one of the tasks of the educator is also to provoke the *discovering* of need for knowing and never to impose the knowledge whose need was not yet perceived. Sometimes the need is just felt—is that right?—but not yet perceived. There is a difference.

THIRD PARTY: Right. Would you say that this is something that you have to figure out, that you have to reinvent or figure out every moment that you're in a relationship with a student?

PAULO: Yes. I would tell you that a good teacher is the teacher who, in being or becoming permanently competent, is permanently aware of surprise and never, never stops being surprised. Do you see? One of the worst things in life is to stop being surprised. This is why Myles is a child! Always we have to look. Today suddenly a flower is the reason for your surprise. Tomor-

row, it may be the same flower, just with a different
color, because of the age of the flower.

"Pockets of hope": Literacy and citizenship

THIRD PARTY: Please talk about Highlander's citizenship
schools and the early literacy work in Recife. What's
striking me is that you were both in different places
working with community groups, Paulo working in Recife and Myles working in Johns Island, both finding
new ways of doing literacy based on a concept of social
change. How did you arrive at that process?

MYLES: In the process of talking about the Citizenship
Schools, I would like not just a comparison but an
evaluation of how we went at it. First, we had been
having workshops at Highlander in the fifties about
the problem of segregation in the south. Highlander
always tried to remind people that they are part of the
world and they have responsibilities and opportunities
to do things outside their own communities. It's rather
amusing in a way, and significant, that the Citizenship
School idea first was talked about at a workshop on
the United Nations. Esau Jenkins, a black man from
Johns Island, South Carolina, came to Highlander with
Septima Clark, a schoolteacher who had come to Highlander herself from Charleston, South Carolina.

Esau Jenkins said at this international workshop that
he thought it was fine to talk about the world but that he
had problems at home. His problem was to get help on
teaching the people on his island to read well enough to

pass the voter registration requirement exam that was given by white registrars who were very unsympathetic to blacks voting and used the restriction of literacy as a means of keeping blacks from voting. He said he'd been trying to teach people to read as they rode on his bus. He had a bus service about thirty or forty miles into the city from the island, bringing domestics, factory workers, his black neighbors to work. On the bus he had a captive audience, and he tried to teach them to learn about reading on the trip. He was the recognized leader in that island in terms of problems of the people, and like a lot of black people he preached every once in a while.

One of the things Highlander had always done was to say to people: "Highlander's our base, but if you try to do something and need some help, we'll respond to your request for help. We won't go into anybody's community or organization as an expert, but we will come in and try to help you with your problem." So it was in response to his invitation that we went to Johns Island.

I decided I'd spend some time with Esau and with Septima and try to learn what I could about Johns Island. I lived down there with Esau for awhile, two or three weeks at a time. I would talk to the people at work, fishing, and growing rice. They still grew some rice, which they harvested by hand, but most of them— even though they all had little pieces of land—most of them made their living working in the big plantations or in the city. They were dependent on working for somebody else for a living. They spoke Gullah, a mixture of English and African, maybe a little French, and I had to get my ears accustomed to understanding it.

While I was trying to get acquainted, I explored the past efforts for people to get literacy training, get schooling. I found out from Septima, who had taught there, that they'd had very, very poor schools, and I found out from my own investigation that there had been people trying to teach literacy classes on that island for years, since the Civil War. I met two people who told me that they couldn't get anybody in the island interested in learning to read and write, that they had tried for years. They'd start and drop out, and there was no interest. I found unspent federal money and unspent state money for literacy.

So obviously there was a problem and it was quite simple. Literacy workers were not treating these people with any kind of respect. The kind of programs they were offering was an insult to them. These older people, adults, had to sit in little desks for children. The children laughed and called them "granddaddy longlegs." So there was a good clue as to what *not* to do. That started me on a line of thinking that was very simple. How do you treat people with respect? How do you do a program that treats people with respect? I was sure that they would have the motivation. It's easy enough to get people to want to vote who have never had a right to vote and who have been denied that right, and in a place where there's mostly black people, to eventually have a majority of the vote.

So the basis of the program was one that would

respect people. It became quite obvious that the education would have to be done in an out-of-school setting because the schools were a "granddaddy-longlegs" memory. So the first thing to do was to try to find a way to have educational programs outside the schooling system, and the next thing was to find out what kind of people would be good teachers in a school that showed respect. To be on the safe side—although Septima differed with me a little bit about this and she was a schoolteacher (you might have differed too, Paulo)—we finally decided we wouldn't have any certified teachers, anybody who had been trained as teachers. Trained teachers would have to be thinking in terms of what they had learned, methodology, and they would identify illiterate adults with illiterate children. They would have a tendency to want to teach the same subject matter in the same way that they taught children.

Then there was the problem of the tendency of white people everywhere to dominate black people. You could eliminate that problem very simply by not having any white people teaching. These conditions for learning were the first things that we agreed on. When I say we, I mean Esau, Septima, and me.

The other thing we talked about in advance was *what* the people would learn to read, since they had only a short time to do it. We couldn't start out with little simple things, simple words, because they had to learn to read in a short period of time a very long, wordy section of the South Carolina law that had words in it they'd never heard of before, words that most of us had difficulty pronouncing. We had to start closer to where the people had to end up in a short period. That meant that we'd have to find some way for their motivation to enable them to grasp rapidly rather complicated sentences and big words.

Who can we get to teach? Bernice Robinson, a young black woman, Septima's niece, had been to Highlander and was impressed. She'd worked in New York and other places, but she was back in Charleston. She hadn't quite finished high school, but she was very bright. She said Highlander is the place we can really learn. "If there's anything I could ever do to help Highlander, just let me know."

So we said: "You can help by teaching other people. You've got part of a high-school education"—she was way beyond that in her thinking—"but most of all you care for people. You know how to get along with people and you inspire people. You know you don't feel superior." So she finally reluctantly agreed. For the first time in her life, she thought of herself as teaching others, but she *had* been teaching people things. She had been teaching young people how to sew. She ran a black hairdresser's establishment, a beauty parlor, but unlike white beauty parlors, a black beauty parlor is a cultural center. It's a place where people come to talk about things, and in that economy that's a status position. She was sophisticated in a lot of ways. But her willingness to do that was based on her love for her own people and wanting to be helpful.

Bernice started out without any plans or anything. We wanted her to get acquainted with the situation and let her own thinking come out. I know Septima wanted to give her a lesson plan to start with, and I objected to that and Esau agreed with me. Bernice started by telling students: "I'm not a teacher. I really don't know why they wanted me to do this, but I'm here and I'll learn *with* you. I'll learn as I go along." That was her attitude.

After she got started, she called me and asked for a poster, the Declaration of Human Rights, that was up on the wall when she was a student at Highlander to use as a primer. That was her idea, because she was beginning to understand that she had to challenge these people. Although there were big words, it wasn't *just* big words that they had to learn to read in the South Carolina Constitution. At that time Highlander had a statement of purpose that told what Highlander was about. Bernice thought that had some good ideas about democracy and about citizenship, so she asked for a copy of it too. That was one of the things they learned to read. It was that level of material that she used in her teaching, but mostly it was just getting them to practice writing their names, writing, filling out money orders. They wanted very practical sort of things, so she built the program around what they wanted, what they asked for.

In the meantime they were all trying to get the chance to vote because she organized that class of about twenty-five people into a community organization. It wasn't a literacy class. It was a community organization. They were already talking about what they were going to do when they got to vote. They were talking about using their citizenship to do something, and they named it the Citizenship School, not a literacy school. That helped with the motivation.

She had more people who ended her class than started. Eighty percent of the total number passed our examination. Our examination was for them to go down to the courthouse and register to vote. So when the registration board said they had the right to vote, we said they'd passed the examination. Eighty percent of them were able to do that.

We thought only in terms of one school, and if that worked, maybe we'd do it again right there. Within a week or two, they asked for other schools in other parts of the island, and Bernice ran another school. We hadn't thought beyond what she could do herself. But by that time demands were coming in so fast that we decided to let other people do the teaching and not just let Bernice do all the teaching. It was getting beyond our original expectations. So what we did was to have these other teachers apprentice to her. We hadn't organized a system of spreading the Citizenship School idea.

Before the third school was over, there was request for a Citizenship School by the people in Edisto, the neighboring island, and a request for Daufuskie, still further south, down in Georgia, as well as other requests. We set up a kind of a training program for Citizenship School teachers at Highlander. Bernice was the head of it and Septima was an adviser. By that time Septima had been put in charge of directing the organizing of Citizenship Schools. Bernice selected her own staff to train new teachers. She picked four teachers who had been apprenticed to her, the ones that she thought would be the best to train other people. In other words, from Bernice on, there was nobody who wasn't trained by the people that Bernice trained. So we kept passing on from person to person as much as you can pass on. The only person who had any training in education—the only person with a college education, for example—was Septima, who was the director of the whole program.

That was the framework in which we set up the schools. The program started in January of 1957, and by 1961, there had been over four hundred teachers trained, and there'd been over four thousand students. The voters in these areas had gone up about 300 percent. It was a success in terms of what it set out to be. We spoke earlier of the idea of Highlander being one in which we dealt with a very few people intensively, and their job was to go back to their communities and multiply what they had learned. Well this was our most successful multiplication of an idea. It spread in all directions because it had a lot of dynamism in it. And as it went along, the original idea that Bernice had developed became only part of the procedures that we used because everybody was adding. Some would come from the teachers, some would come from the students. Their program was being enriched, and it got more and more effective as it went along. There wasn't a single Citizenship School teacher who was connected with Highlander. They weren't on Highlander staff. The only people on the Highlander staff were Septima Clark and Bernice Robinson. The rest of the people were on their own.

74

Now this program later on got so big that it was bigger than everything else we were doing at Highlander. It was an inexpensive program. We didn't pay teachers. There were no salaries involved. We financed the training but we didn't finance any of the actual teaching. The community was responsible for that. And none of them worked for pay. They were all volunteers, black people teaching black people. That organization became so big, spread so fast, and was involving so much of our time and attention that we decided we'd do like we had done before. We'd had two or three other programs that we had evolved back in the labor period that got big, and unions took them over. We didn't want to spend time on operating a successful program. Anybody can do that. We'd try to experiment and develop something else. We decided we wanted to spin off the Citizenship Schools. It was well enough established that somebody else could do it. At that time we brought Andrew Young, who was later U.S. ambassador to the United Nations and is now the mayor of Atlanta, to Highlander to coordinate the spread of this program. Before he got here, Martin Luther King asked if we would work out a program for Southern Christian Leadership Conference. Septima kept telling him about the Citizenship School program. At first I didn't think that would necessarily be the best program for them, but later on King got interested in that program, and I got to thinking maybe after all it was the best program for them, and it would certainly solve our problem, getting it off our hands. And after quite a bit of discussion, they decided that they would make that their official program. When they did that, Andy and Septima decided they would go with the program and help establish it in sclc, Southern Christian Leadership Conference. They had a much broader base than we had. By that time the civil rights movement was beginning to get started. It moved from Montgomery to Atlanta, and the idea was spreading. The Citizenship Schools became the program for the Southern Christian Leadership Conference, and they made adaptations but it stayed pretty much the same program.

Andy Young and other people think of it as kind of basic to the civil rights movement, and I think it's one of the basics, but I think there are others. That program succeeded at a time that no other literacy programs were succeeding in the United States. And at the time, when it cost as much to teach somebody to read and write as it did to send them to Harvard for a year, we were doing it for less than one hundred dollars a person in actual costs. It was done in a three-months' period on the average, two long nights a week, and the success stayed about the same in terms of 75, 80 percent of people going through the program being able to register to vote.

Now there's no question it worked. It worked and spread. I'd like to talk about what you did, but I'm interested in what the elements were, how you would see these elements that I've been talking about.

PAULO: Well, first of all, I think that it's interesting for us as educators, to think again and again about the political atmosphere, the social atmosphere, cultural atmosphere in which we work as educators. It was in your experience, we can see that. I don't believe in programs for adult literacy that just are organized by some educators in some place and afterwards are offered to illiterates all over the country. It does not work. I remember that in 1975 there was an international meeting, in Persepolis, sponsored by UNESCO in order to analyze some reports made by UNESCO, evaluations of programs all over the world in adult literacy. I was in that meeting with Soviets, Americans, Latin Americans, Europeans, Asians, the Chinese, Vietnamese, and Koreans. One of the conclusions that was put in the final report (Statement of Persepolis, if I'm not mistaken) was that the programs of adult literacy have been efficient in societies in which suffering and change created a special motivation in the people for reading and writing. It was before the Nicaraguan revolution. The Nicaraguan revolution was the last example for that. The program Myles talked about was made without revolution. I say no. I am not making reference exclusively to revolution that gets power. The political connotation, the aspiration of freedom, of creativity was there among the black people. That is, the motivation was there among the people.

The people wanted and needed to read and to write, precisely in order to have more of a possibility to be themselves. That is, the people wanted to write and to read at that time because they knew that they were being prevented from voting because they could not read and write words. Then we can see the coincidence: on one hand, the people needing, wanting; on the other hand, you and the team, open to the needs of the people. Because of that, you could start without too much preoccupation concerning methods and techniques and materials because you had the principle ingredient, which was the desire of the people, the political motivation of the people. For the people at that moment, getting reading and writing was really an important instrument and also a sign of respect for them, self-respect.

Another thing that I feel is very important in your explanation and report of this beautiful history is how Bernice multiplied the program—that is, how it was possible, starting from Bernice, to multiply Bernice without courses with lots of theoretical introductions! This is one of the terrible things we do. Sometimes we put fifty people to be trained in how to teach illiterates, and we spend fourteen days speaking about different theories and matters, and the teachers cannot *experience* it. Then the last day we have a lunch together, and the next day the teachers meet the illiterates and don't know how to work. In this case Bernice prepared for future educators by teaching in their presence. It's beautiful because she taught through her example.

One thing is not clear for me. I think that you said two years later there were about two hundred teachers. Did all these two hundred come to Bernice or did the ones who were trained by Bernice multiply also?

MYLES: After two or three training programs run by Bernice and her staff, the demand became so great. Up to that time there had been no manual written and no methods written, just word of mouth. So many people were asking about it that they decided they'd write something up. It was also decided that we would tape a five-day training session. Bernice didn't tell her teachers what we were going to do with it. She said just go ahead and pay no attention to it. We were afraid that if we told them we were going to turn this into a manual, they'd become self-conscious. We just wanted them to teach the way they had been teaching and the people learning the way they'd been learning. Transcribing the tapes and making the manual was a long tedious job done by Ann Romasco, who was on staff at the time.

Now we figured that would be as authentic as you could get. We made a manual out of what they had already said. No one wrote or spoke anything specifically for the manual. They were saying it to teach and help peers learn, because this was kind of peer teaching. (These people who were the teachers were not any better educated than the people they were teaching. Quite often the people who were learning had a much better education than the people who were teaching, but they were not our Citizenship School teachers.) The transcribed material was put together in about a thirty-page manual. It was the only thing that was ever written while the program was at Highlander.

After the program went to the SCLC and began spreading so fast, they put out other kinds of manuals and study guides. Septima continued to work on that, but we didn't want to get away from the creativity and the originality that stemmed from Bernice. So as long as it was at Highlander, there wasn't any disconnection. Now when it got away from Highlander, when it got broader, then they not only used manuals but the idea had spread so widely in the South that people were beginning to start Citizenship Schools of their own.

That's when I was really excited. I was down in Mississippi, back in the country one day, and a woman came up to me and she said, "What do you do?" I said, "Well, I'm a teacher." She said: "I'm a teacher, too. I teach at my house. I'm a Citizenship School teacher. Do you know what that is?" I said, "Tell us." She said: "Well, you know I started this. This is my idea. We're going to make citizens out of people. I'm teaching them to read and write. I went to the fourth grade, and I'm teaching people to read and write. When I get through with this one, some of my neighbors want to start one." I said, "That's just a wonderful, wonderful idea. Do you think anybody else knows about this idea?" She said, "No, but they will."

She had taken this idea and internalized it, and here she was starting her own. I was so excited about this. I asked her if she was having any problems of any kind. She said that they didn't have enough pencils and paper and things like that. I gave her ten dollars to buy pencils. She needed no more help than that. She needed no white guy, no money, nobody else to come. All she needed was a little money for pencils, and that was all she needed. Now that was when I felt the program was successful, when it was no longer even part of an organization.

PAULO: Myles, two questions. The first is, do you remember how Bernice worked with the Declaration of Human Rights in order to make it possible for the illiterates to begin to grasp how to read and to write?

MYLES: She read it to them and she told them that she had seen it at Highlander. It said what she believed and some of the things that she thought they believed, and she thought they'd like it. So she read it and they responded to it, of course, because it spoke in terms they could understand, international world freedom, liberation. They wanted to be able to read it because they liked it and because it made a lot of sense to them. She didn't try to carry everybody along, to have everyone read it. She didn't work on the basis that everybody had to be doing the same thing. They were doing what was interesting. And she said in the end they'd all want to learn to read it because if some of them did it, the others would want to do it. So she just took the ones that wanted to do it, and they learned as much as they could on it and then the others came in. It wasn't just something that was done, and then that was a class, and then the next time it was something else. It was mixed in with learning to read and write their name, filling out money orders, doing a little of a lot of things. She wouldn't try to have a plan for it. It stayed kind of spontaneous.

THIRD PARTY: Did she break the words down and build other words or did she teach the reading word-for-word?

MYLES: No. She didn't do that. She didn't know anything about that.

PAULO: It's not a syllabical language. After some time the people could read, could write. Do you see the power of interest, of motivation?

MYLES: I'm not suggesting she couldn't have done better if

she'd known a lot more things and had a lot more ideas, not at all. She did well enough without knowing these things.

PAULO: And did you think about some postliteracy program?

MYLES: Oh yes.

PAULO: Tell me something about it.

MYLES: Well, after the people were able to vote, Esau Jenkins who was the father of this idea, said, "We're going to have to have a second stage program." He called it a second stage. "We're going to have to follow up on the literacy schools, on the Citizenship Schools, and we've got to help people understand how they can use their vote more intelligently and get them interested in running for office. We got to talking about what we were going to use our power for when we get it, schools, health. We want to talk about the overall struggle for justice." The civil rights movement was beginning to take shape, and he wanted to be part of that. Now there's a study made of this program by Carl Tjerandsen.* He was executive secretary of a foundation that gave us some money and he wrote in detail. I guess his study has more detail of this than anyone else's, and he describes the second stage.

You know what it reminds me of. It reminds me of popular education following the literacy crusade in Nicaragua. It's a step beyond, using the same people.

---

* Carl Tjerandsen, *Education for Citizenship: A Foundation's Experience*, (Santa Cruz, Calif.: Emil Schwarzhaupt Foundation, 1980); see excerpt in *Convergence* 15, no. 6 (1983): 10–22.

No, that was just the beginning. There wasn't any thought of that being an end in itself. It had a purpose, but reading and writing wasn't the purpose. Being a citizen was the purpose. So once you could read and write, then the class moved on to other things, and incidentally (and this was incidental because it wasn't planned but it doesn't mean it's not important), they had to keep on reading and writing to do the things that the second stage required them to do.

PAULO: It should be interesting if it was possible sometime for Highlander to bring together some of those who learned how to read and write thirty, thirty-five years ago. I think that it should be a beautiful moment.

Last month I met four ex-illiterates from the first work I did in Brazil. I had lunch with them and a friend of mine who worked with me at São Paulo at that time in 1964 before the coup d'état. They still read and write.

I love to see the coincidence between our experiences, Myles, but it's not the same. The circumstances were different. The culture is different. The historical moment was different. I was in Brazil, Myles here. Without knowing anything about Myles, I was increasing an old search that I had started in the fifties. In 1961, specifically, I was searching for something in the field of literacy. In the fifties I had started to work seriously with people, with workers, peasants, fishers, trying to learn from them how to work with them. Elza used to go with me to every place, and she watched me working. Afterward, she made corrections and she called my attention to ways I could improve, and we discussed. I said no, I am not wrong, and she said yes, you are! (Sometimes two days later I would discover that I was.) In the fifties I was learning how to work with people. I was thinking critically about education, general education. I was making some theoretical reflections about education. I was thinking about what I did as a teacher of syntax, for example. In the beginning of 1960, I began to look more directly, specifically, for something in the field of literacy, of adult literacy. One of my political motivations was that illiterates could not vote in Brazil. Here in the United States, illiteracy was a good justification for racial discrimination. In Brazil it was also, but above all it revealed class—social class—discrimination. In Brazil, whether white or black, the illiterate could not vote. Now the illiterates can vote but cannot be voted on, cannot run for office. It's a contradiction. They have the right to vote, but they cannot run for election. One of my dreams was fighting against this injustice, to make it possible for illiterates to learn quickly how to write and to read, and simultaneously learn also the reasons why the society works in this or that way. My main preoccupation was this.

There is another coincidence. I also started this work outside of the schools, nevertheless without denying the importance of the schools. I remember that, for example, instead of naming a school for adults, I named the space and the students and the teacher "Circle of Culture" in order to avoid a name that sounds to me too much like traditional school. Instead of calling the teacher "teacher," I named him or her "coordinator of discussion, of debate, dialogue." And the students I called "participants of discussion."

It's interesting also because, for example, Bernice started using the Declaration of Human Rights. Look, I was not there, but I am sure that at the moment in which Bernice showed the Declaration of the Human Rights to the first group and she said what it was, I am sure that there was a discussion about that.

MYLES: Oh yes.

PAULO: I'm absolutely sure that the problems of human rights, discrimination, racial exploitation, liberation, freedom—all these things—came up. We were not there in the exact moment at which she worked, but I am sure that there was that, precisely because the people came to Bernice's course because they wanted their affirmation, because they needed to fight in favor of their dignity. The Declaration of Human Rights ought to have been to them a fantastic proof, a justification that they were right in fighting. They were right in wanting to get the right to vote. In the last analysis, in my terminology, Bernice used the Declaration of Human Rights as a codification. It was, yes, a codification, and when she showed the declaration to them, the *debating* started. I am so sure that I speak like this. The debating started, and based on your experience today, I think that you agree with me when I say something that I did not see but that I think happened.

MYLES: Well, you're right on that. I mentioned the fact that they organized themselves as a community organization. They continued to meet after that as a community organization.

PAULO: Yes.

MYLES: The teaching stopped and the community education started. The blacks were the ones who named it a school. The blacks were the ones who called people "teacher." They called it a Citizenship School, and they had a teacher. To them that was real education. That was their terminology, not mine or Bernice's.

PAULO: It is beautiful. I am seeing now as if I were there in that exact moment: that by discussing with Bernice some points of the declaration, they were reading the world and not yet the words of the declaration. They were starting a different reading of the world mediated by the Declaration of Human Rights and possibly in this rereading, through the understanding of the Declaration of Human Rights, they were discovering things, knowing new knowledge. That is, they were confirming some already known knowledge and knowing something different. In other words, through the experience with Bernice they were going *beyond*.

MYLES: I remember now that Bernice said some of them asked, "What does that word mean?" And she'd have to explain the meaning of some of the words. But she said they all knew what the total thing meant. She says they understood it in totality, but they didn't understand some of the words.

PAULO: And it is beautiful, this movement. Before writing the words and reading the words, they were rereading their reality and they were preparing themselves to write the words in order to read them. It's impossible to read the words without writing them. That is, reading implies writing. Then at some point they began to do better. I also used the codifications for that. I used the codifications differently.

86

THIRD PARTY: Paulo could you talk about how and why you developed the codifications?

PAULO: Yes it's interesting. I have said something also about that in other places, where community activists and students drew pictures to describe their concepts of education, but I think that it is historical. I have to repeat. For me the question, theoretically, was like this: I was convinced that we would have to start from some very, very concrete piece of people's reality. Inside of the representation of some aspects of this reality, I would put the first word or the word that I call the generative word. In a syllabical language like ours, this word can be split, and afterward we can make combinations with the syllables.

The codification has a task, a role, in the process of learning and of knowing. It's very interesting how we worked yesterday in the workshop, where community activists and students drew pictures to describe their concepts of education. We used another language, pictures, to try to find the normal language that is used. We drew and then we made codifications. I found it very interesting.

In my case, the codification works as a challenge, a challenge to the students and the educator. Then the codification gives itself or exposes itself to the cognitive subjects, to those who are open to know, in order for them to read the codification without any kind of word, just a representation of the reality. Precisely because the reality you presented in the codification is the reality of the students, in looking at the codification, the students see again what they already know about reality. Then they speak about what they are seeing, and in speaking about what they are seeing, they are expressing how, before that moment, they perceived the reality. Is it clear? Reading the codification leads people to have a perception of the former perception of the reality. That is, in some moment I perceive as I was perceiving before, the same reality that now is being represented in the codification. In doing that, maybe I change my perception.

Let us think as an example. Give a camera to several people and say: "Record what you want to record, and next week we meet together. The only demand I have is that each group has to justify to all of us the reasons why the group preferred to record, for example, the front of the school, the market, the church." You can discuss with the group, video by video, trying to grasp the contents of the reality. They were reading through the camera. They were reading reality through the camera. The camera is a reader of reality, but now it's necessary for us to go into deepening the reading made through the camera in order to put another language in that and to discuss with the group lots of issues that are behind and sometimes hidden. The codification helps the educators and the students to do that. It is a mediation to the discussion. Because of that, the codification was not something to help exclusively the educators. That is, the codification was not an instrument for helping the teacher in his or her speech about the content. The codification is an object to be known, and to the extent that codification represents a part of the concrete reality, in trying to understand or to describe the codification, you are again trying to understand the concrete reality in which you are.

At some point we stop discussing the global aspects, and we get the word, the generative word. For example, if the first word is *favela* (which means slum in English), you have a picture of a *favela* with the word written, *favela*. After discussing the sociological and political dimensions of that—they know very well because they live there—you get the word *favela* and you start a new job, which is the job of decodifying the word, as you did, for example, with your experience. This is one of the advantages of a syllabical language like Portuguese and Spanish. English is not like this.

MYLES: No, you can't do that in English.

PAULO: That is, *favela* has three syllables. Then you have lots of possible combinations. *Favela* makes it possible to create these twenty or thirty new words on the first night of the experience. You see the similarities? Bernice used the declaration as a codification also, in order to discuss with the people.

Bernice talks* about the happiness a woman experienced when she could write for the first time. It is as if I were in Brazil twenty-four years ago. It is as if I were now in Brazil because I am reading now about explosions of happiness among illiterates who have begun to write and to live. It's Latin America also. It's the world.

---

*   Descriptions of the Citizenship School may be found in Sandra Brenneman Oldendorf, "Highlander Folk School and the South Carolina Sea Island Citizenship Schools: Implications for the Social Studies" (Diss., University of Kentucky, 1987).

Bernice says: "I never will forget the emotion. I laughed when she got up, took the ruler out of my hand, went up to the board and said 'There is my name. Anna. There is my last name.' Goose pimples came out all over me!" What is for me important now in commenting is this: It's impossible to be an educator without having the possibility this woman had at this moment, to be reinvented. Because in the last analysis she was born again by Anna.

MYLES: That's right.

PAULO: The moment in which Anna discovered her name has such an importance in our lives. We already forgot that you are Thorsten and I am Paulo. It is obvious for us, but for the illiterate, it's not obvious. She was Anna. She continued to be Anna. But at the moment in which she could write "Anna," she found another dimension of herself. She found a piece of her identity. There is another very important thing here that Bernice speaks about. Sometimes an illiterate used to write an X as if it were his name. When he really discovered that his name was the other one, he did not want it. He said, "No, my name is this." And he rejected the real name because it was not an X.

MYLES: X was his name.

PAULO: Bernice speaks about how she worked. She says very clearly that it is very important to get the document, the authorization for voting [voter registration]. Because of that, it was very important for the illiterate to learn how to read and to write and then to take the examination and to get registered. She says yes, it is very important, but what is really important is to know why to vote and for whom to vote. When she said that, she became very clear. Politically speaking, I think that if we take Bernice's experience of life and of knowing, we see how practice, when we think of it, really illuminates us and gives us the possibility to go on. Bernice learned lots of things in teaching, and she discovered the importance of what I call constantly "political clarity." The question was not exclusively to teach how to read and to write but to challenge future readers concerning how to use the right to vote.

Perhaps I am naive. In order for us to be more and more critical we need to recognize some naiveties. But when we look at the history of human beings, we see how we in the world are still having to walk a lot in order to become more human. Because when we think that these things Myles spoke about, the struggle for blacks to read and to write; when we read that this fantastic man Jenkins, a great educator in being a driver who created a school in the back of a bus in order for the people to learn, it was yesterday. Yesterday. At the same time, in Brazil we had discrimination. I am speaking here not as a Brazilian but as a human being just recognizing how much we have to do still all over the world in order to try to reinvent the world. It is incredible to see how the blacks were and continue to be so prevented from being.

MYLES: I was asked by the state director of adult education, who is in charge of the literacy program, to do a workshop with Sue Thrasher here at Highlander, to talk about the Citizenship School as an example of using a group approach as against an individualistic approach.

He's determined to have the programs in Tennessee done in groups and not by individual tutoring, and he was wanting our help in getting people to switch over from their individualized teaching to group process. In the workshop, we were struggling all day to find an equivalent or parallel situation. You can't have the equivalent of a Cuban situation, Nicaraguan situation, or the Highlander situation. There's no equivalency today to any of those programs. What is it that would provide this basis for people having the motivation to learn? How would you use that group process today? It was really challenging to me to try to discuss with that group. I was unsuccessful in finding from them what they would consider equivalence, and I had to end up just by challenging them to find out what to use as a basis. They're at a disadvantage in that we were working in really a revolutionary situation. And they're in a low ebb-tide situation, where the going practice is to fall back on telling people that if they learn to read and write they'll get a job. I said, "Anybody that's dumb enough to believe that is too dumb to learn to read." But yet they still tell poor people that. Now to get from that level to a place where you have some kind of group motivation seems to be the challenge of the day here in this period. How would you deal with that?

PAULO: I agree with you. For example, your experience as well as my experience in the sixties in Brazil did not happen in the air. They happened in some historical space, in a context with some special historical, political, social, cultural elements in the atmosphere. Now possibly you would not get the same results. This does not mean that you could not get similar results in some areas of the country, at some times.

In some states of Brazil today we have progressive governments, and in some municipalities all over the country we have very good people working seriously. In all these situations, it is possible to reorganize adult literacy, to reorganize education and health, lots of popular education in the broader meaning of this word. I am helping as much as I can in different parts of the country, but I don't see a possibility today for a national campaign. The time is changed.

MYLES: No, I don't see in this country a national campaign of significance. The government is trying to launch a literacy campaign without having any reason for it except that it'd be a good thing if people could become literate. There could be found pockets in the country where you could have successful literacy programs, but just to assume it anywhere and everywhere. . . . I think the poor and the people who can't read and write have a sense that without structural changes nothing is worth really getting excited about. They know much more clearly than intellectuals do that reforms don't reform. They don't change anything. They've been the guinea pigs for too many programs. Now if you could come to them with a radical idea—like we were able to tie into in the Citizenship School program—where they see something significant, they'd become citizens of the world. Then they'll identify with that, but not with short-range limited objectives that they know from experience don't get them anywhere. They won't invest much time or energy in it.

93

So to embolden people to act, the challenge has got to be a radical challenge. It can't be a little simplistic reform that reformers think will help them. It's got to be something that they know out of experience could possibly bring about a change. And we sell people like that short by assuming that they can take a little baby step and isn't this wonderful. If they can see something that's challenging, something that they believe would change things for them, and if they can see a path that they could move on towards that goal, then I think something can be done. But that kind of analysis doesn't fit the national situation in any way here in this country. So it leaves us working with the remnants, leaves us working with the little pockets of hope and adventurism wherever we can find it. That's why I say you can't have a national literacy campaign.

THIRD PARTY: Do you see those pockets of hope now? What are they?

MYLES: As you've heard me say, I'm not out in the situations where I know well enough what's going on. Finding the pockets is not an intellectual process. It's a process of being involved. The reason I think Highlander could function back when there was something happening is that we were working through our people who came to Highlander and helping them in getting out in the field and just dealing with people. Just knowing what's going on, we were able to sense places where there's a potential for radical social change. I use the word *potential* because it wasn't there. But since I'm not out there, not in touch with the situation like I was at one time, I don't know. From reading or talking or hearing anybody talk, I don't see any place now that I would say you could build a radical program. When I say I don't know where these pockets are, it doesn't mean that they aren't there. It means that I'm not close enough to the situation, not sensitive enough to it, to find them. It's always hard to find.

The only way these pockets can be found is to get outside the traditional sort of things that everybody else is doing and identify with these people—in terms of their deep knowledge—that limited reforms don't help. I had to spend a long time down in Johns Island before people would really confide in me and talk to me so I could get a feel of where they were. I'm sure that in all times in history there are little places where things are beginning to develop, but I don't think you can arrive at that intellectually or by making surveys or taking polls or things of that kind.

Paulo, you've spent a lot of time in this country. What's your sense of what I'm talking about? I'm both pessimistic and optimistic. I think the potential is there, but I don't think we've found it.

PAULO: Yes, I agree with you. But I think that after these hours of talking, we can see easily how education implying political decision can never be an act of voluntarism. Do you see? For me it's very important for this to be known, to be felt. We need the political decision for that, but we cannot make it just because we want to. This is the question of the limits of education.

MYLES: History gets in your way. History gets in your way.

CHAPTER 3

Ideas

"Without practice there's no knowledge"

PAULO: I ask: Do the people have the right or not, in the
process of taking their history into their hands, to develop another kind of language as a dimension of those
who have the power? This question has to do with an
old one. For example, do the people have the right or
not to know better what they already know? Another
question: Do the people have the right or not to participate in the process of producing the new knowledge?
I am sure that a serious process of social transformation of society has to do that. Of course, it implies a
change in the way of producing economically. It implies a much greater participation of the masses of the
people in the process of power. Then it means to renew
the understanding of power. Of course, I agree with

Myles that the people have a kind of language that is organic knowledge . . .

MYLES: People's knowledge.

PAULO: . . . people's knowledge, in which the body has much more place than in our way of thinking and of knowing. As progressive teachers and educators, we have first to get the knowledge about how the people know. You say it very clearly in your Danish article, Myles. It means then to understand the way they speak, their syntax, their semantics. Then secondly we have to invent with the people the ways for them to go *beyond* their state of thinking.

MYLES: That's a starting place, not the ending place.

PAULO: Well, then yes. It's a starting and not a staying point. Because of that I come back to the question again of reading texts. I started also recognizing the fantastic importance of the way the people think, speak, act— the design of it all. Then I have to understand the experience, the practice of the people. But I also know that *without practice there's no knowledge;* at least it's difficult to know without practice. We have to have a certain theoretical kind of practice in order to know also. But practice in itself is not its theory. It creates knowledge, but it is not its own theory.

Secondly, in discussing my practice with the people as an educator, I have to know something more than the people know. At least I have to understand better theoretically what is happening in the people's practice.

Reading is one of the ways I can get the theoretical illumination of practice in a certain moment. If I don't get that, do you know what can happen? We as popular educators begin to walk in a circle, without the possibility of going beyond the circle, without going beyond man's theory of why we do not go beyond. Do you see? It has to do with a very important moment in theory of knowledge, which is knowing man's moment of information.

MYLES: And a theory of what you're going to do.

PAULO: Yes. Information can be got through reading a book, and it can be got through a conversation. That is, I hope that this conversation between us here can help tomorrow when it becomes a book, can help a student in Brazil, Africa, or here, or another country of Latin America when he or she reads us. Maybe he or she has a certain problem and says, "Look maybe here is the explanation of my obstacle. There is a theory."

MYLES: Someone criticized Highlander workshops, saying, "All you do is sit there and tell stories." Well, if he'd seen me in the spring planting my garden, he would've said: "That guy doesn't know how to garden, how to grow vegetables. I didn't see any vegetables. All I saw was him putting a little seed in the ground. He's a faker as a gardener because he doesn't grow anything. I saw him and there's nothing there." Well he was doing the same thing about observing the workshop. It was the seeds getting ready to start, and he thought that was the whole process. To me, it's essential that you start where people are. But if you're going to start where they are and they don't change, then there's no point in starting because you're not going anywhere. So while I insist on starting where people are, that's the only place they could start. *I* can start somewhere else. I can start where *I* am, but they've got to start where *they* are. But then if you don't have some vision of what ought to be or what they can become, then you have no way of contributing anything to the process. Your theory determines what you want to do in terms of helping people grow. So it's extremely important that you have a theory about it that helps you decide.

For example, when I was the director of Highlander I was involved in deciding who it is we would work with. To decide who to work with was based on our theory of who was important. My way of thinking was to ask if they are people who are working on structural change or on limited reforms. If they're working on structural change and we can find some people there to work with, then we'll choose to work with that group. If we didn't have that theory of dealing with structural problems instead of limited problems, then we would have chosen the opposite. So there's no way you can keep people just going around in a circle. You can't have a spiral, you'll just have a circle that stays flat, if you don't have a theory about where you're going. The problem is where does that theory come from. Is that a valid theory? The only way you can answer that is to test it out, as far as I know.

PAULO: The educator must know in favor of whom and in favor of what he or she wants. That means to know against whom and against what we are working as educators. I don't believe in the kind of education that works in favor of humanity. That is, it does not exist in "humanity." It is an abstraction. Humanity for me is

100

Mary, Peter, John, very concrete. Then I need to know in whose favor I am trying to work. It means the political clarity that the educator has to have. Respecting the knowledge of the people for me is a political attitude consistent with the political choice of the educator if he or she thinks about a different kind of society. In other words, I cannot fight for a freer society if at the same time I don't respect the knowledge of the people.

To repeat myself, I would say that we have to go beyond the common sense of the people, with the people. My quest is not to go alone but to go with the people. Then having a certain scientific understanding of how the structures of society work, I can go beyond the common-sense understanding of how the society works —not to stay at this level but, starting from this, to go beyond. Theory does that.

MYLES: Theory does that only if it's authentic.

PAULO: Yes, yes, but the theory is always becoming. For example, you started this morning talking about how you are constantly changing. Nevertheless you are the same. This is precisely—

MYLES: Dialectical.

PAULO: Yes, yes, yes! This is precise because knowledge always is becoming. That is, if the act of knowing has historicity, then today's knowledge about something is not necessarily the same tomorrow. Knowledge is changed to the extent that reality also moves and changes. Then theory also does the same. It's not something stabilized, immobilized. You are right!

"Is it possible *just* to teach biology?"

MYLES: When I first started thinking about the relationship of learning and social change, it had nothing to do with Highlander. It was years earlier when I was debating with myself this whole idea of neutrality. Academicians, politicians, all the people that are supposed to be guiding this country say you've got to be neutral. As soon as I started looking at that word *neutral* and what it meant, it became very obvious to me there can be no such thing as neutrality. It's a code word for the existing system. It has nothing to do with anything but agreeing to what is and will always be—that's what neutrality is. *Neutrality is just following the crowd.* Neutrality is just being what the system asks us to be. Neutrality, in other words, was an immoral act. I was thinking in religious terms then. It was to me a refusal to oppose injustice or to take sides that are unpopular. It's an excuse, in other words. So I discarded the word neutrality before I even started thinking much about educational ideas. Of course, when I got more into thinking about educational ideas and about changed society, it became more and more obvious that you've got to take sides. You need to know why you take sides; you should be able to justify it. And those were early learnings, so that cleared that way.

   The next step is to figure out what to do. As I said earlier, I decided long before that I wasn't interested in being good, I was interested in being good *for something*. That leads you to make an analysis of society. That's when I was helped by some of the things I learned from

Marxism about analysis and about the practical use of the whole business of conflict, how you deal with the dichotomies or seeming dichotomies. That was an act of trying to learn how to analyze society. I started trying to learn about society so I could make a moral judgment, a rational judgment. That was the basis of finally deciding that I was going to work with poor people, working people. That's the basis of deciding if I was going to side with what we later on started calling Third World countries. I didn't have any names for them but it was the same, my position hasn't changed.

I remember I got some clarification from Niebuhr's lectures, which ended up in his book *Moral Man in Immoral Society*. I was in his class when he was working on it, and he practiced his values on us. So I was influenced by the thinking, the clarification that went into the book—that it's the structures of society that we've got to change. We don't change men's hearts. So it was in Niebuhr's class that I first really clarified in my own mind, my own thinking, the idea that it doesn't make a great deal of difference what the people *are;* if they're in the system, they're going to function like the system dictates that they function. From then on I've been more concerned with structural changes than I have with changing hearts of people.

PAULO: Neutrality. This is why neutrality is the best way for one to hide his or her choice, you see. If you are not interested in proclaiming your choices, then you have to say that you are neutral. But if in being neutral, you are just hiding your choice because it seems possible to be neutral in the relationship between the oppressors and the oppressed, it's absolutely impossible. It's the neutrality vis-à-vis this kind of relationship that works in favor of the dominant.

MYLES: Always.

PAULO: Then instead of saying I am with the dominant, I say that I'm neutral.

Myles, I would like to put this on the table: Precisely because it is impossible for education to be neutral, educators have to confront some practical problems. A biology teacher must know biology, but is it possible *just* to teach biology? What I want to know is whether it's possible to teach biology without discussing social conditions, you see. Is it possible to discuss, to study the phenomenon of life without discussing exploitation, domination, freedom, democracy, and so on. I think that it's impossible, but I am also sure that if I am a teacher of biology, I must teach biology.

Then my question is to clarify the role of the teacher. I said biology, I could say history of education. I could say philosophy, theology, and mathematics, and so on. This role is a problem for the teachers. It has to do with their competency, with their political clarity, with their consistency and their understanding of the very process. It's not a question for the biology teacher to impose on the students his or her political ideas. Do you see? But it *is* a question for the teacher to discuss the issue in a broader way and even to express his or her *choice*. Do you see, then? It is a problem of not being neutral, but of how to be different.

MYLES: And not impose your ideas on people. I agree fully that you have the responsibility to put whatever you're teaching in a social context, relating it to society not just acting as if it had nothing to do with people, with humanity, because it does. There's no science that can't be used for good or for evil. Science could be used by whoever has the power to use it and desire to use it. If you make people knowledgeable about these sciences and don't point out this fact, then you're saying, I withdraw from the battle, from the discussion of the ethics involved. I just stick to the facts. And that of course means that you've surrendered to the strongest forces. You say you're neutral in what you do, you aren't that concerned with it. If the Pentagon is using your discoveries, that's not your problem. It's unavoidable that you have some responsibility, it seems to me, regardless of what you teach or what your subject is or what your skill is. Whatever you have to contribute has a social dimension. And I think it's ineffective to try to *impose* that on anybody. Sharing it with them is one thing, but trying to impose it is another. You honestly say these are my ideas and I have a right to my opinion, and if I have a right to my opinion then you have a right to your opinion.

You can't have an individual right. It has to be a universal right. I have no rights that everybody else doesn't have. There's no right I could claim that anybody else in the world can't claim, and I have to fight for their exercising that right just like I have to fight for my own. That doesn't mean I have to impose my ideas on people, but it means I have a responsibility to provide whatever light I can on the subject and share my ideas with people.

People sometimes say they're afraid to do that for fear they'll impose their ideas on people. You know, I remember that this same discussion came up back several years ago, talking to some of my friends and former colleagues at the University of Chicago. They said I was always advocating democracy and decision making when I was a student, campaigning for the rights of dissidents to express themselves. They said, now here you are, you're imposing your ideas on people who come to Highlander. I said, "Do you impose your ideas?" "Oh, no we're very careful not to impose our ideas." And I said, "Well, you have one problem I don't have. You're such powerful teachers that if you even breathe what you believe, it would influence everybody. I don't have that problem. I've always been glad I could get somebody to pay attention to my ideas, just to share them with them. I don't have to worry about being so overpowering that everybody will take everything I say for granted." Well they didn't appreciate that very much, but I did make my point.

PAULO: Yes.

MYLES: I do think if I have an idea, if I believe something, I've got to believe it's good for everybody. It can't be just good for me. Now if I believe that I've got some *reason* for believing it, and I've come to that belief by a lot of processes—we've talked about some of them already— then I have a right to assume that other people, if they were exposed to some of the things I've been exposed to, if they had some of the learning experiences I've had, they might come to that same conclusion. So I'm going to try to expose them to some ideas, some learning that was mine, in the hopes that they will see the light. If I didn't believe that, I wouldn't think it was very important what I believe. They've got to come at it from their own way. I don't see any problem with taking a position.

Now as a matter of strategy, I very seldom tell people what my position is on things when we're having discussions, because I don't think it's worth wasting the breath until they ask a question about it. When they ask about it, I'm delighted to tell them. Until they pose the question that has some relevance to *them*, they're not going to pay any attention to it. I just think that's not a good way to function educationally. I don't have any problem about this imposing on people.

PAULO: This is one of the theoretical questions we have when we have a grasp on education. It is complex, you know. For example, if we think that there is no education without educators, that there is no education without students, then there is no educational situation without certain objects to be known, to be taught, to be learned. I prefer to say to be known and reknown. There is no education without objectives that go beyond this situation today. We have methods to approach the content, methods to make us get closer to the learners. Some methods of approaching students can in fact push us very far *from* the student. The educational situation demands methods, techniques, and all this together constitutes a process, or implies a process. The teacher must command the contents of the program. The question is to know how to build the program, how to choose the contents, who has the power to choose the program.

What is the way to organize the contents. Who says that A, B, and C must be known? Who declares that the students know nothing? Who says that the teachers do not have the duty to know what the students already know when they come to the classroom? All these things in my point of view must be answered. I am sure that there is no possibility for the existence of a teacher who does not teach. That is, the teacher of something has to *teach* something. The teacher does not need just to know the contents but also to know *how* to teach the contents. To know the history of the content and not exclusively the content.

Now I come back again to the question. First of all, I don't separate the content as a scientific object from its historical and social context—as you said before, the social conditions in which I am teaching the content to the students. On the one hand, I know that I cannot leave the content in a parenthesis and just speak with the students about the political situation of the country, because the students come to me to learn biology, for example. If I put biology in a parenthesis to say Brazilian politics are terrible now, the students have the right to say, but look Paulo, we came here to study biology. I can't do that. But on the other hand, I cannot put history and social conditions in parenthesis and then teach biology exclusively. My question is how to make clear to the students that there is no such a thing named biology in itself. If the teacher of biology does that and the teacher of physics does that and so on, then the students end up by gaining the critical understanding that biology and all the disciplines are not isolated from the social life. This is my demand. These two risks exist: the risk of putting in parenthesis the content and to emphasize exclusively the political problem and the risk of putting in parenthesis the political dimension of the content and to teach just the content. For me both attitudes are wrong. And it is a question that comes up because of the nature of the process of education or the process of politics.

"I've always been ambivalent about charismatic leaders"

MYLES: Now charismatic leaders operate not on a small-group basis like I do or like a teacher does. They operate in terms of huge chunks of society where there's no way to get a feedback, no way to get interaction with the people. You can intuit it or you can feel it; there's ways to get the feedback, but it's indirect. There's where I think there is danger of imposing on people, because their emotions are involved. In education, emotions are involved but they're a part of a whole package including intellect. In charismatic leadership, sometimes *only* the emotions are involved, and I think there is a danger of people, either good or bad people, getting converts on the basis of not really understanding what it is they're going into. I've always been ambivalent about charismatic leaders. The charismatic leaders that I differ with I have no problem with. The charismatic leaders that I agree with, like Martin Luther King or Malcolm X, I have to take a different attitude toward. It's a little different when they're my kind.

One time I took a leave of absence from Highlander to organize textile workers, in the beginning of the industrial union movement in 1937. I was a successful organizer. I had two thousand people and their families that were mobilized. To keep them occupied and to keep solidarity, we had big mass meetings every night. The average attendance was two thousand. We were covered by the highway patrol, police, radio, and every newspaper; it was a big show. In an effort to really hold the thing together—to mobilize, that's the word—I used to make speeches and put on a program. We'd have music and singing, and I'd talk. I went through the repertoire! I talked about all the labor history I knew and all the world history I knew.

In the process of mobilizing a crowd, I kind of got a sense of power, because the people were with me and the enemy was against me. You get those two things going and you're sure you're on the right track. I was enjoying it, and suddenly I realized: "What the hell am I doing? What is this?" I never will forget it. I was alone in my hotel room, and I was thinking about this feeling of power. I was a little scared of it, and yet I was fascinated by it, because it was an experience I'd never had before. I remembered that when I was a kid, before we went to bed, we had to kneel down beside the bed and say our prayers. The prayer was "lead me not into temptation"—not "deliver me from sin." I thought, "If you yield to temptation, that's too late. You're already hooked, so your prayer ought to be to keep out of temptation." This temptation was scary, so I backed off. I decided I wasn't going to stay the whole year as an organizer. I decided to get back to education, because I was afraid of power of this kind. Not that I was good at it, but I was good *enough* at it that it scared me. I decided I wanted to be an educator not an organizer or speaker.

On the other hand, I worked pretty closely with Martin Luther King. I had great respect for his charismatic leadership. I know there's a real role for this type of leadership, but I have a problem with it. Much of the problem you raise about educators is multiplied many times with charismatic leaders. But I don't know how to analyze that. I've never really come to grips with that. How do you feel about this charismatic leadership?

PAULO: I agree with your analysis. But I have the impression also that no one is charismatic. Someone *becomes* charismatic in history, socially. The question for me is once again the problem of humility. If the leader discovers that he is becoming charismatic not because of his or her *qualities* but because mainly he or she is being able to express the expectations of a great mass of people, then he or she is much more of a *translator* of the aspirations and dreams of the people, instead of being the *creator* of the dreams. In expressing the dreams, he or she is recreating these dreams. If he or she is humble, I think that the danger of power would diminish.

The charismatic leader needs to know that finally he was not created by God and afterward sent as a package to save the people. He discovers that in order to save the people, it is necessary that he also saves himself. In your words, he or she has to discover that salvation demands first liberation. Liberation and salvation are *social* events and not individual ones. The leader has to understand that he's been shaped *by* the mass of the people also and is not only shaping the people. For example, I think that Martin Luther King was like this. Malcolm X also. They were not, as far as I understood them, far from [the will of] the country. They had different ways to be strong because they *had* to be strong. In spite of that, they did not appear as the exclusive owners of the truth. They had something to strongly denounce and to announce. If the charismatic leader is not able to criticize but at the same time to announce what should be, he loses the *prophetical* dimension that is necessary. The question is not just to make the criticism but to interpret the dreams of the people who are making the leader become charismatic.

MYLES: And if they don't realize that the people are making them, and think they're making the people . . .

PAULO: Yes, this is the danger.

MYLES: That's the danger. Neither King or Malcolm X thought they were making the people. They knew that they were trying to give voice to the people making them. They had that saving grace.

THIRD PARTY: I want to base this on practice again. During the civil rights movement, Martin Luther King was one of many charismatic leaders that Highlander dealt with. How difficult was this really to put into practice on a day-to-day basis at Highlander? What were the problems with always reminding yourself of this way of practicing, especially during a time like that when on the one hand you had many charismatic people, and on the other, another way of exposing people to ways of learning?

MYLES: That question is fairly easy to answer. Highlander wasn't just the recipient of the speeches of the charismatic leaders. Highlander was involved in the Citizenship School program, which was an integral part of the civil rights movement. What we had done before was being used as one of the many bases of the civil rights movement. So our role was an accepted, functioning role within the civil rights movement. We had our own sense of values, sense of importance. Andy Young has characterized the Citizenship School as the basis of the civil rights movement, and other people have said it played a major role in the civil rights movement. I think it played only *one* of the roles in the civil rights movement. We had enough of a role that we could be satisfied with our own role. For example, we were asked to set up an educational program for the Southern Christian Leadership Conference. We were asked to set up an educational program for the Student Non-Violent Coordinating Committee. I had no desire to play any other kind of role, except a background educational role. It was very fulfilling and very satisfactory. We knew we were involved in our own way and that our role was valued by the charismatic leaders. I think there is a full recognizable role where you don't have to feel inferior in any way to the charismatic role. We were dealing with the radicals, but we were dealing also with the people that they couldn't reach. They had to reach the people through us quite often. Their speeches didn't get to them. And when they did, the people didn't know what to do with the speeches. The charismatic leaders respected us because we could implement their speeches.

In the labor movement, for example, the international presidents of the unions wanted to come to Highlander and make speeches, because it gave them a certain appearance of being educators. But we didn't have time for those speeches. We wanted them to send the students to Highlander and pay the bill, but we didn't want them to come to speak, but they insisted. One time I remember we decided we had to give in to this, but we didn't want it to take too much time, so we decided to invite five officials at a time, for one day of a workshop that lasted two weeks. They could say they'd been to Highlander, and we didn't have to put up with their speeches so much. I never will forget. One of the old timers said, "In the time that has been allotted me, I can do no more than to give my name and part of my address." And he meant mailing address not speech! We recognized that we had to have union officials' support as part of our process, but we didn't expect to educate them. They didn't come to be educated. They came to *be* there, be present. So we gave them a chance to say they'd been at Highlander and write it up in their newspapers. When we had Martin Luther King here, we had him to speak. We had him at our twenty-fifth anniversary to make a speech. We didn't try to make those speeches into discussions.

The staff understood that. We all worked those things out together, but we did have problems among ourselves. I remember one time I was holding forth in one of the workers' sessions. A student sent a note up to me saying, "When you're talking, you aren't learning."

They sent the note to *me*! I was talking, you know. So we had to deal with those problems.

"The difference between education and organizing"

MYLES: One of the unsolved problems, even I think here at Highlander, is the difference between education and organizing, and that's an old question, it goes way back. Saul Alinsky and I went on a circuit. We had the "Alinsky/Horton show" that went out on the circuit debating and discussing the difference between organizing and education. At that time Saul was a staunch supporter of Highlander, and I was a staunch supporter of him, but we differed and we recognized the difference. We had no problem about it, and we tried to explain to people that there was a difference. Saul says that organizing educates. I said that education makes possible organization, but there's a different interest, different emphasis. That's still unclarified. In my mind I kept them separate because I could function much better having a clear cut idea about what I consider the difference in operating on that basis.

The reason it was such a debatable subject is because the overwhelming majority of the people who were organizing and who were officials of unions in the South had been at Highlander. So the public who only saw that didn't know what went on at Highlander, and they assumed that we were an organizer's training school. But I kept saying no, no. We do education and they become organized. They become officials. They become whatever they are, educational directors. Basically it's not technical training. We're not in the technical business. We emphasize ways you analyze and perform and relate to people, but that's what I call education, not organizing. When I wanted to organize—which I did at one period, something I'll go into later on—I resigned from the Highlander staff. I took a leave of absence from the Highlander staff because I didn't want organizing and education confused in the minds of the people. It was confusing enough as it was.

So Highlander's been in the situation where we were looked at from all kinds of different angles. We always had to watch not to accept the appraisal of other people, and try to make our own criticism relating to these critics. We just had to constantly keep clear about what we meant by education. One of the examples I used to use got me in trouble and still gets me in trouble when I use it. I'd say if you were working with an organization and there's a choice between the goal of that organization, or the particular program they're working on, and educating people, developing people, helping them grow, helping them become able to analyze—if there's a choice, we'd sacrifice the goal of the organization for helping the people grow, because we think in the long run it's a bigger contribution. That's still a hot issue. I used that illustration in a participatory research meeting when I was pushed on the difference. One woman there was organizing a hospital. She was just furious, because she thought it was inhumane to take that position, that my purpose was to develop people instead of particular issues. I would usually find there wouldn't be that contradiction, you see, but if it came down to it, then you have to make that distinction. That's how strongly I felt about separating the two ideas.

PAULO: Could I make a comment just about that. I think that mobilization of masses of people has or had, inside of itself, organization. That is, it's impossible to start mobilizing without organizing. The very process of mobilizing demands organization of those who are beginning to be mobilized. Secondly, I think that both mobilizing and organizing have in their nature education as something indispensable—that is, education as development of sensibility, of the notion of risk, of confronting some tensions that you have to have in the process of mobilizing or organizing. Knowing, for example, the dialectical relationship between tactics and strategy. You have to have some tactics that have to do with the strategy you have. You understand the strategy as the objective, as the goal, as the dream you have, and as the tactics you raise as you try to put into practice, to materialize the objective, the dream. In the process of mobilizing, of organizing, you need from time to time to stop a little bit with the leaders in the groups in order to think about the space you already walked. In reflecting on the action of mobilizing and organizing, you begin to teach something. You *have* to teach something. It's impossible for me not to learn. A good process of mobilizing and organizing results in learning from the very process and goes beyond.

Until some years ago, among the left groups and left parties, we had strong examples of how education was not taken seriously during the process of mobilization and organization, which were seen just as political process. In fact they are *educational* processes at the same time. Why this attitude? I think that the answer should be found in the analysis of or the understanding of education as something that really is superstructure and a productive reproducer of the dominant ideology. It's very clear, for example, in the seventies, the writings about education's power to reproduce the dominant ideology. It was, I think, because of this that the left parties and the groups always thought, in Latin America, for example, that education is something that comes *after*, after we get power. When we get power through the revolution, then we can begin to treat education. In this line of thought, this vision was not able even to make a distinction between the schooling system as Myles has underlined and the activities *out* of the subsystem. In fact, nevertheless, even education inside of the subsystem of education is not exclusively the reproducer of the dominant ideology. This is the task that the ruling class expects the teachers to accomplish. But it's possible also to have another task as an educator. Instead of reproducing the dominant ideology, an educator can denounce it, taking a risk of course. It's not easy to be done, but education cannot be exhausted exclusively as the reproducer of the subsystem of the dominant ideology. Theoretically it is not exclusively this.

Today I think that the tension is expressed in a different way. I know many people in the left parties in Latin America who discovered through practice what political education is. I think that the tension is being treated in a different way today. When we're in the process of mobilizing or organizing, it begins to be seen also as an educational problem of process and product, because undoubtedly there is a different kind of education in mobilization before getting power, and there is also the continuity of that. That's a mistake committed before, that education should come just exclusively after organizing. Education is *before*, is *during*, and is *after*. It's a process, a permanent process. It has to do with the human existence and curiosity.

MYLES: If you're into having a successful organizing campaign and dealing with a specific project, and that's the *goal*, then whether you do it yourself or an expert does it or some bountiful person in the community does it, or the government does it without your involvement because that solves the problem—then you don't take the time to let people develop their own solutions. If the purpose is to solve the problem, there are a lot of ways to solve the problem that are so much simpler than going through all this educational process. Solving the problem can't be the goal of education. It *can* be the goal of organizations. That's why I don't think organizing and education are the same thing. Organizing implies that there's a specific, limited goal that needs to be achieved, and the purpose is to achieve that goal. Now if that's it, then the easiest way to get that done solves the problem. But if education is to be part of the process, then you may not actually get that problem solved, but you've educated a lot of people. You have to make that choice. That's why I say there's a difference. So when I went to organize for a union, I got a leave of absence from the

Highlander staff. I wouldn't do that as a member of the
Highlander staff because I don't think organizing and
education are the same thing. I do think participatory
research and education are the same thing, but I don't
think organizing and education are the same. I think
the goal is different.

Now a lot of people use organizing to educate
people. That's what I was trying to do when I was organizing textile unions, but when it comes down to it, I
wasn't free to make a decision not to get a contract, to
sacrifice the contract and the organization for education, because I was hired to organize the union. Organizers are committed to achieving a limited, specific
goal whether or not it leads to structural change, or
reinforces the system, or plays in the hands of capitalists. The problem is confused because a lot of people
use organizing to do some education and they think it's
empowerment because that's what they're *supposed* to
be doing. But quite often they *disempower* people in the
process by using experts to tell them what to do while
having the semblance of empowering people. That con-
fuses the issue considerably.

THIRD PARTY: Your description of organizing is a description of what most of education is. Most of education is
specifying a specific objective and reaching that objective irregardless of how the process works.

MYLES: That's right. Schooling.

THIRD PARTY: So most schooling is in fact analogous to what
you call organizing?

PAULO: But, inside of the process of organizing, as Myles
said, first we have education taking part of the nature

of organizing. What I want to say is that it's impossible to organize without educating and *being* educated by the very process of organizing. Secondly, we can take advantage of the process of organizing in order to develop a very special process of education. Maybe I will try to be more clear. For example, when we are trying to organize, of course we have to try to mobilize, because mobilization and organization are together. But in the process of mobilizing and automatically organizing we discover as well, as in any kind of action or practice, that we must become more and more efficient. If you are not trying to be efficient in organizing workshops, the people will not answer you next year when you call. That is, efficiency, without being an instrument of enslaving you, is something that is absolutely necessary. Inefficiency has to do with the distance between what you do and what you would like to get. Do you see that we manage with efficiency in this place? I have my dream. Then what did I do in order to materialize my dream? Then my evaluation has to do with this.

Those who are engaged in mobilizing and organizing have to evaluate this process. In the process of evaluation, undoubtedly, there is an interpretive and necessary moment in which the leaders who are trying to mobilize and organize have to know better what they are doing. The organizers engage in critical reflection on what they did. In doing that the leaders start participating in a process in the next stage of mobilization and organization, because they change. They tend to change in their language. Do you see? If they don't do that they are not capable. They will change their language, their speech, the contents of their speech to the extent that in mobilizing the people they are learning from the people. And then the more they learn from the people the more they can mobilize. It's expected. They can mobilize the people. Then because of that I always see that it's absolutely necessary for mobilizers and organizers to be quite sure about the educational nature of this practice.

In a second aspect we can show, in an analysis of the process we call mobilizing and organizing—which implies organizers getting more and closer contacts with groups of people—that the organizers are engaged, if they are good, in a kind of participatory research.

THIRD PARTY: If they're good.

PAULO: If they are good. It's necessary to say, if they are good. And if they are good in being involved in participatory research, they necessarily are grasping some issues that have to do with the expectations and frustrations of the people, some issues that have to do with people's lack of knowledge. Then it should be possible, starting from the process of mobilizing, to begin to create workshops, for example, for the people in which educators could illuminate the issues coming from the people. I see too that through educational moments in a mobilizing process, one takes part in the very process of mobilizing. The other one is something that comes up from, and because of, the mobilization process.

MYLES: Yes. I think certainly you can learn from mobilizing, but you can learn to manipulate the people or you can learn to educate the people. There's two kinds of learning that come out of the same experience. In

both the civil rights movement and the labor movement, there's no other identifiable source that produced
as many organizers as Highlander did. There were so
many organizing in the labor movement who came from
Highlander that people called it an organizer's school.
There weren't many organizers in the South. We were
starting without much experience, so we had to develop a lot of organizers. I always said that Highlander
was not a school for organizers. It was a school to help
people learn to analyze and give people values, and they
became the organizers. The reason so many of Highlander's people were successful organizers was because
of that. Not that we trained them in techniques of mobilizing and organizing, because we didn't do that. The
same training that people got to be an organizer, they
got to be an official of the unions, they got to be a committee member, they got to be a shop steward. It was
all the same. It wasn't technical. We didn't tell people
how to do things. But they became successful organizers, and people who wanted to be organizers knew they
came from Highlander, so they'd come to Highlander
so they could be organizers. We taught them our own
way, and the reason we did that was because we wanted
them to be educators as well as organizers. Instead of
just mobilizers we wanted them to educate the people.
They were the people who insisted on having the educational program in their unions. When they'd organize
the union, they'd immediately set up the educational
program because they understood that was part of a
union, whereas some of the people would operate from
the top. They didn't want an educational program be-

cause they wanted to control it from the top. Now that was a different kind of organization. When I say the difference between education and organizing, I don't mean to say you can't have educating and organizing because that's what we try to do. An organizing experience can be educational. It can be. But it has to be done with the purpose of having democratic decision making, having people participate in the action and not having just one authoritative leader. Otherwise it won't work.

I'm not critical of organizations. In fact Highlander is based on organizations. In the old days, for example, we wouldn't take anybody at Highlander who wasn't a product of an organization, who wasn't involved in an organization, who didn't come from an organization. So to separate Highlander's thinking from organizations is a mistake, because we think organizations have to be the first step toward a social movement. What you do in that organization is different if you just think of organizing or if you just think of the way Highlander works. It's a little confusing, but in practice it seemed to work out pretty well.

PAULO: Organizers who hope to educate must increase their historical and cultural sensitivity. An educator or mobilizer without that vigil should change professions. Secondly, without the sensitivity of intuition, it's impossible to become an educator, but it is also impossible to become an educator by stopping at the level of sensitivity. I must be intuitive, but I cannot stop with intuition. I have to take the object of my intuition as an object of my knowing and grasp it theoretically and not because it just exists, you see.

Myles, I remember that some time ago you talked to me about a difficult situation you had in the thirties with a worker-leader who wanted you to say what they should do. Do you remember?

MYLES: We had been successful at Highlander earlier in organizing a county in which we lived, organizing the unions, and organizing the county politically. We took over the county politically by using education, so I knew how to do that. I knew how education could be used as a means of building organizations, union and political organizations, but I didn't know what you could do in a short period of an organizing campaign, which has for its purpose getting a union organized and getting a contract. That's the purpose in setting up a union.

Within that framework I was interested in going as far as I could in helping people develop the capacity to make decisions and to take responsibility, which is what I think is the role of an educator. One of the things I was doing was working through committees to get the committee members to take the responsibilities and learn how to do things. We had a relief committee that needed a little help at first in how you handle relief problems and funds that come in. I finally got this committee and the others to the place where I didn't even need to know what was going on, and I felt that was kind of a measure of success. If they didn't come to me to ask me or to tell me, then I thought they're doing pretty well. But the strike committee was one of the toughest; they had to think through the strategy of a strike. We had the local police force, the county sheriff, the state militia against us. So it was a tough job. They were trying to break the strike. The highway patrol had begun to usher scabs through the picket lines and they were beginning to really break into our solidarity. The strikers said: "We've got to try something new. We've got to do something." One guy said, "Why don't we just dynamite the damn mill?" "Then we won't have a job," they said, "that won't work." We were having a little meeting up in my motel room. There were very few places we could meet where we wouldn't be listened to. The room was probably bugged, and the telephone was. They kept throwing out ideas, and I'd raise questions to get them to think a little more about it. Finally they said they couldn't come up with anything, any strategy, or anything to do. They were getting desperate. They said: "Well, now you've had more experience than we have. You've got to tell us what to do. You're the expert." I said: "No, let's talk about it a little bit more. In the first place I don't know what to do, and if I did know what to do I wouldn't tell you, because if I had to tell you today then I'd have to tell you tomorrow, and when I'm gone you'd have to get somebody else to tell you." One guy reached in his pocket and pulled out a pistol and says, "Goddamn you, if you don't tell us I'm going to kill you." I was tempted then to become an instant expert, right on the spot! But I knew that if I did that, all would be lost and then all the rest of them would start asking me what to do. So I said: "No. Go ahead

and shoot if you want to, but I'm not going to tell you."
And the others calmed him down.

PAULO: This is a very beautiful story, if you consider that the
educator has to educate and then because of that, the
educator has to intervene. When I speak about intervening, some people symbolize this as if I, the educator,
should come with some instruments to cut trees, and so
on. For me it's a fantastic example of how the educator
radically educates.

MYLES: Sounds a little radical all right.

PAULO: The best way you had to intervene was to reject
giving the solution and secondly to be honest. Say first,
I don't know; and secondly, if I did know I would not
tell you because doing it the first time means I would
have to do it the second, third, the fourth. You see, it
is the intervention of the educator. That is, you did not
reject being the educator. It is beautiful.

MYLES: That's why I make the distinction between organizing and educating. Now an organizer's job, one who
wasn't an educator, would be to get that contract the
best way he could. That wouldn't have been a problem
for him—to tell them what he thought was the best way
to deal with that situation. His purpose was to get the
organization's goal achieved, you see. And that's what
an organizer's job is. An organizer's job is not to educate
people as a prime consideration. His job is to accomplish a limited, specific goal. I'm not saying it isn't a
wonderful goal for the people. I'm not saying it isn't
valuable. I'm just saying there's a difference between
organizing and educating, and I think there's a very

important distinction. And an educator should never become an expert, and an organizer quite often finds that that's his main strength, being the expert.

"My expertise is in knowing *not* to be an expert"

THIRD PARTY: Myles, is that sort of the same philosophy that you and Highlander used to exclude people from workshops who the people perceive as experts? I know we've had very similar discussions around other ways that people perceive authority. For instance, in the occupational health movement, when coal miners came to Highlander to learn about and talk about occupational disease, we didn't want doctors in the room. Is there something similar at work here between experts and charismatic leaders doing the same thing in a workshop process?

MYLES: I think we've had a lot of experience with that. Often when I say you start with people's experience, people get the point that you start and stop with that experience, but of course all of you know better. There's a time when people's experience runs out. I'll give you an example. We were working with a group of black parents here in a Tennessee town where only about 5 percent of the population is black. The schools had merged. They weren't integrated; they just absorbed the blacks and made whites out of them without schools changing any of their all-white, racist ways of doing. So the black kids were miserable. The parents at first insisted on them fitting in, and then they finally realized what they were doing, really brutalizing the kids by setting up situations in which they were discriminated against. So they came down to Highlander for a couple of workshops about this situation. They decided that they were going to have a lawsuit, go into court. Well, pretty soon they exhausted what they knew. At that point, I said, "Would it be helpful if we got a lawyer, a friendly lawyer, to tell you the processes you'll have to go through?" They said, "We'll welcome that." Now that's what I call an extension of their knowledge, their experiences, which stays well within the framework of where they are in their thinking. It's their idea. So at that point you can feed in a lot of information that they don't have.

I asked a friend if he could come out—as a teacher, not as a lawyer—to teach them about what having a lawsuit meant in terms of time, cost, likely results and so on. When he got through, they realized that the solution could be ten years off, because there could be appeals, and their kids would be out of school by the time that was over. It would cost a lot of money and, in the meantime, they would more or less just sit on their hands and do nothing. So it would in fact kill their organization. Now he was very sympathetic. He was very pro-integration and he was anxious to be helpful and what he did was extremely helpful. But he wanted to go ahead, go on and advise them about what to do. I stopped him at that point because I didn't want the expert to tell them what to do. I wanted the expert to tell them the facts and let them decide what to do. Now there's a big difference in giving information and telling people how to use it. I had to really just get a hold of him by the arm and lead him out of the room. He was still talking over his shoulder when I was taking him out. He still wanted to help these people out.

Now that use of expert knowledge is different from having the expert telling people what to do, and I think that's where I draw the line. I have no problem with using information that experts have, as long as they don't say this is what you should do. I've never yet found any experts that know where the line is. If people who want to be experts want to tell people what to do because they think it's their *duty* to tell them what to do, to me that takes away the power of people to make decisions. It means that they're going to call another expert when they need help. They learn by doing what you're supposed to do, and there's no empowerment that comes as a result of that. There is an organizational success, maybe, as a result of that, but there's no *empowerment* of people, no learning. So that's my feeling about how you use and how you don't use experts.

THIRD PARTY: You could probably predict that this would come up. Why did you wait to bring the lawyer into the circle? Why wasn't he there from the beginning?

MYLES: Sure I knew it would come up. It had to come up, because I know the pattern in this region is you go into court and you lull people. But suppose I had said the first day that these people came to Highlander: "Now I know you're going to end up tomorrow talking about a lawsuit. We're going to get a lawyer out here and get this settled at once and let him tell you what to do." Then there'd be no learning taking place. There'd be some information shared, but no learning—no learning about how to deal with problems, no sense of responsibility.

They would learn that way to turn their problems over to an expert. People already do that all the time; they don't need to come to Highlander to turn things over to the expert. They've got to think through the information themselves or they can't use it when they get back. It can't be part of their experience, their experience of learning, and therefore be theirs, if you deny them the right of making it theirs. If I'm the expert, my expertise is in knowing *not* to be an expert or in knowing how I feel experts should be used.

"My respect for the soul of the culture . . ."

PAULO: How is it possible for us to work in a community without feeling the *spirit* of the culture that has been there for many years, without trying to understand the soul of the culture? We cannot interfere in this culture. Without understanding the soul of the culture we just invade the culture.

I think that it's necessary to clarify a point. I come back again to a question you [third party] asked us, in which you said you and Myles are demanding concerning vision and values. I come back again with a very good example now. My respect for the soul of the culture does not prevent me from trying, with the people, to change some conditions that appear to me as obviously against the beauty of being human. Let me give a concrete example. Let us take a main cultural tradition in Latin America that prevents men from cooking. It is very interesting to analyze that. In the last analysis, men created the tradition and the assumption in the heads of the women that if men cook, they give the impression that they are no longer male. With that, men get advantages. Okay, this is the tradition. Let us take the second community in which men do nothing concerning the home work. Women have to do everything at home and also in the field, and men come back from the field just to eat, but the women also have been there working.

Now I am an educator, and I am discussing in workshops with this community. My question is this: is it possible for me, concerning my vision of the world— because I respect the cultural tradition of this community—is it possible for me to spend my life without ever touching this point? Without ever criticizing them just because I respect their traditional culture? No, I don't do that. But I am not invading in not doing that—in doing the opposite, that is, in criticizing, in challenging men and women in this culture to understand how wrong it is from the human point of view. One man told me that it is determined historically that all men have the right to eat what women cook. It's not like this because it is a kind of distinct destiny. It is cultural and historical, and if it is cultural and historical, it can be changed. And if it can be changed, it's not unethical to put the possibility of change on the table.

It's just one example, and there are lots of other examples concerning respect. I insist it is one thing to respect; the other thing is to keep and to increase something that has nothing to do with the vision of the educator. I prefer to be very clear and to assume my duty of challenging, but of course I know that I have the duty

to challenge that culture and those people. I also know
that there is a time to start doing that. I cannot start
on the same day I arrive. I cannot do that. Then the
question now is not strategical, it's tactical. Strategically
I am against it. I am in favor of the struggle of women.
Tactically I can be silent six months about this, but the
first occasion I have, I bring the issue on the table, even
though it makes us uncomfortable.

MYLES: Paulo I'd like to get back to where we started on this.
Now I'm all for those of us who are honest about our
positions, who say we're against the system. We want
to change the system. I'm all for us being extremely
critical with each other about this problem. I have no
respect for people who claim to be neutral or for institutions that claim to be neutral making criticisms of us—
none. They have the power base to magnify all of their
positions, and then they label it neutral.

PAULO: I remember how Amilcar Cabral, the great African
leader, dealt with this. In *The Letters to Guinea Bissau*,* I
discussed a little bit how Amilcar dealt with this. During
the war in the bush, he always led seminars. He brought
some people from the front with him to the bush. In
the shadows of the trees, he used to discuss, to evaluate the war, but he always brought some issues about
science, culture, teaching to discuss with the people. In
one of the seminars, one of the issues he touched was
the power of the amulet. He said: "One of you told me
that you were saved because of your amulet. I would

---

* Paulo Freire, *Pedagogy in Process: The Letters to Guinea Bissau*, trans.
Carmen St. John Hunter (New York: Seabury Press, 1978).

like to tell you that we save *ourselves* from the bullets of the Portuguese, if we *learn* how to save ourselves. I am sure that the sons of your sons will say sometime our fathers and our parents fought beautifully, but they used to have some strange ideas." He respected his culture but he was fighting against what he used to call the weakness of culture. He said, in his reflections about culture, that every culture has negativeness and positiveness, and what we have to do is to improve the positiveness and to overcome the negativeness. The belief in the power of the amulet was one of the weaknesses of the culture. It would be absolutely wrong if he said those who believe in the amulet will be in jail for two days. It would be an absurdity, but for me it should be also an absurdity not to have said what he said.

MYLES: He had to find a way to do it.

PAULO: Yes.

MYLES: We had to find ways to handle our own "weakness of culture." One of the real problems in the South in the early days of Highlander was segregation, discrimination against people of color, legally and traditionally. One of our principles is that we believe in social equality for all people and no discrimination for any reason— religious, race, sex, or anything else. The social customs were to have segregation. Now how did we deal with that social custom? The way that was used by most people working in what then was called race relations was to talk about it and pray over it and wait for magic changes, I suppose. Some dealt with segregation by having segregated programs, and educating Blacks here and whites there, like it was traditional to do. We chose to deal with it directly, knowing that a discussion and analysis wouldn't change their minds.

We decided to hold integrated workshops and say nothing about it. We found that if you didn't talk about it, if you didn't force people to admit that they were wrong—that's what you do when you debate and argue with people—you can do it. People didn't quite understand how it was happening. They just suddenly realized they were eating together and sleeping in the same rooms, and since they were used to doing what they were *supposed* to do in society, the status quo, they didn't know how to react negatively to *our* status quo. We had another status quo at Highlander, so as long as we didn't talk about it, it was very very little problem. Then later on, participants started talking about it from another point of view, a point of view of experience. They had *experienced* something new, so they had something positive to build on. When we started talking about it, it wasn't to say: "Now, look you've changed. We were right and you were wrong." We said: "Now you've had an experience here. When you get back you'll be dealing with people in your unions who haven't had this experience, and they're going to know you've been to an integrated school. How are you going to explain it to them?" So they started, not ever talking about how they had changed or how they had faced this problem, but with how they could explain to other people. We just skipped the stage of discussion. Of course, it was going on inside all the time, but we didn't want to put it in terms of an argument or a debate.

Now we were violating the mores. We were doing

something; we weren't taking our time. We just did it, head on, from the very beginning. Sometimes you have to deal with those problems and sometimes you don't. Sometimes you can delay, sometimes you can't. I think you always have to be conscious of going against the traditions of people. You have to really think seriously about that.

PAULO: Absolutely. Even in order to change some traditions, you have to start from there. It's impossible not to.

THIRD PARTY: When you talk about looking at the traditions of a culture, you're saying part of my responsibility is to evaluate the culture, to criticize the culture, to accept and to understand it, but to criticize it. Then part of my responsibility is to take anything that I feel is unjust, unfair and try to do something about it. Isn't that fair?

PAULO: Yes it is.

MYLES: When people criticize me for not having any respect for existing structures and institutions, I protest. I say I give institutions and structures and traditions all the respect that I think they deserve. That's usually mighty little, but there are things that I do respect. They have to earn that respect. They have to earn it by serving people. They don't earn it just by age or legality or tradition.

We've got some good traditions in this country on paper and in the lives of people about individual freedom, which I value very highly. I used to say there are only two things that people who came to Highlander had to accept as a condition of coming, and that is no discrimination, period, and complete freedom of speech. Now freedom of speech in this country, if you want to simplify it, is to me a value to be preserved and extended and built on. It's a tradition that we've developed further than most countries, and I value that. I'd like to see other countries have it. For another example, in the traditions of the Native Americans, we have the holistic concept of society being one, that the universe is one. People and trees and rocks and history are all merged. In Native American visions, they're all related. They have the vision but they know history. This holistic concept is the oldest tradition we actually have in terms of history. It's not widespread, but you can't say it's an *un-American* tradition. It's the most American kind of tradition.

I'm not saying that everything in a people's culture is bad. I'm just saying that you have to pick and choose and keep the good things. Now I have very little respect for the electoral system in the United States. I could have respected it in the early days, when the country was small and we had small population. The system that we have in the United States was set up at a time when the total population was the population of Tennessee. We've stretched it to try to make it work for different kind of problems and in stretching and adapting it, we've lost its meaning. We still have the form but not the meaning. There's a lot of things that we have to look at critically that might have been useful at one time that are no longer useful. I think there's some good in everything. There's some bad in everything. But there's so little good in some things that you know for practical purposes they're useless. They're beyond salvation. There's so much good in some things, even though there's bad, that we build on that.

PAULO: I have the impression in our discussion that we have been getting around a central point. We have said lots of times since the beginning of our conversations, five days ago, that the educator does not have the right to be silent just because he or she has to respect the culture. If he or she does not have the right to impose his or her voice on the people, he does not have the right to be silent. It has to do precisely with the duty of intervening, which the educator has to assume without becoming afraid. There is no reason for an educator to be ashamed of this.

"I learned a lot from being a father"

PAULO: I remember I learned a lot from being a father.

MYLES: So did I.

PAULO: And I learned a lot from watching how Elza was a mother. I remember at home, Elza and I never said no without explaining the reason why. Never. If I said no, I would have to have some reason. Look, I don't want to give you the impression that I am a rationalist. No, it is not true, because I am a very strongly emotional being, full of feelings without any fear of expressing them. What I want to say is that behind *no* and *yes* there is argument and disagreement, and in every kind of argument and disagreement there are many things to be said. I just don't say no because I love you; I say no because I have some reasons to say no. Why not teach kids to begin to look for the reasons, for the facts, for the events, because there always are reasons. I had to explain every time *why* it was not possible.

Secondly, every time it was possible for children, without risking their lives, to learn by doing, I preferred that they do this. And afterwards I discussed it with them. In being a father and a mother, Elza and I were always, it's very interesting, engaged in the process of reflecting with the kids. I hope that they didn't ever get tired of our teaching. We always were teaching them. Because of this, I never said no and was silent. I remember [that] one time I lost my patience; I can't remember where I was. I committed a tremendous injustice with Christina, and she became very sad immediately. She went to bed, and I followed her. I kissed her and I said: "I came here to ask you to forgive me. I was wrong." And she smiled with the lips and the eyes and she kissed me, and she slept very well. I hope that because of that, she did not need a psychotherapist today. Maybe I have avoided this expense.

MYLES: That's wonderful, how much you can learn. I could give a lot of examples, but one example of learning is still with me, and I still use it. Our kids grew up in the mountains, where people sometimes beat and whip their kids. It's called physical abuse, and of course we didn't believe in physical abuse. We didn't believe in whipping the kids and slapping them around, and we were going to be kind to them, love them. One time Thorsten had done something that I didn't approve of, and I talked to him and I told him how that hurt me, how sad I was. Thorsten started crying and he said:

"Why are you so mean to me? Why don't you just do like other parents do and whip me so it'd be over with. It wouldn't be so mean, not so painful." Suddenly, I realized that he would much prefer a switching and get it over with than for me to be sad. It hurt him more for me to be sad than it would for me to whip him. Well, it really upset my whole way of thinking about brutality. I realized here I was being the brutal person trying to keep from being brutal. It's always in the back of my mind when I read about mountain parents switching their kids and about how brutal they are. What they don't say is that kid crawls up in her daddy's lap, even though he hasn't washed his face since he got back from the mine. She hugs and kisses the father because she knows there's love there. They would make the same mistake I made, you know. It's changed the whole way of looking at things, because brutality can be something other than physical. That was a real lesson that Thorsten taught me. A real lesson.

THIRD PARTY: Did he get spankings after that?

MYLES: I'm serious, you do learn so much how to deal with problems. After Zilphia had died, Thorsten and Charis got to doing a little conniving. They came to me one day and said: "You know, it's just wonderful to have you for a parent, and it means so much, all the things that you do at Highlander, things you believe in, people discussing things and voting on things. You say you believe in black and white people living together, so you do what you believe in." They made me this song and dance that we're so lucky to have a parent like you, and I was saying yeah, now what's coming next, what's coming next? They said, "We think we ought to vote on everything we do." It was two to one, you know, and I said, "Well, it'd be good if we could do it. What do you have in mind?" "We've been talking about having a vacation, and you keep saying we can't have a vacation. We ought to vote on it." I said: "You can vote on the vacation and you can decide to do it, and then you can help me get the money to do it, and you can help me arrange my schedule so I'll have time to do it, and we'll take a vacation. But you're going to have to share some of the responsibilities of carrying out the decision. You can make decisions for yourself without doing this, but you can't make decisions for other people. You can't make decisions about what other people have to do."

I had to deal with the problem of making decisions for others in a very important way with the kids. How far do you go and *how* do you go in terms of making democracy work and letting people make decisions? My children educated me in a lot of ways. Some of those ways have carried over.

PAULO: Yes. I think that maybe the main lesson I got in working with my son and daughters was how important it was for their development, for us, Elza and myself, to understand from the beginning the need for limits. Without the limits, it's impossible for freedom to become freedom and also it's impossible for authority to accomplish its duty, which is precisely to structure limits.

But once again your question. You see how important is the problem you brought, Myles, into our discussion, and I know that you brought this problem

141

into the discussion because you experienced it in Latin America, as I have. That is, we need limits, and in experiencing the need for limits, we are also experiencing the respect for freedom and the need for exercising authority. You see, without the authority of the father and of the mother, the kids cannot grow up well. This is not a problem of four times four is sixteen in the decimal system. I am now speaking with the certainty of experience. The same thing is true; without the limits of the teacher, the students cannot know. That is, the teacher has to enforce the limits. For example, how is it possible for a teacher to teach if the students come and go from the room any time they want on the behalf of "democracy." What if the teacher is not able to say on the first day: "no, it's impossible. You come here on time and you leave here on time as well as I do." What respect can the students have for a teacher who never arrives on time and who never gives class because he or she is always trying to make a pact with the students in order *not* to give them the class? A teacher who proposes surreptitiously to the students not to come to the next class does not have any right to demand respect, because she or he lost the limit for his or her authority. Freedom cannot respect this kind of authority and it destroys the relationship. You see? I think that it's very important. The same thing is in the relationship between, for example, power in society and ourselves.

MYLES: There's another side to this limit business. The limits quite often have the opposite effect. They inhibit growth and development. If you use that idea of limits, you've got to also think of how people accept limits that don't even exist—like in the university. Teachers there don't dare question the capitalist system. They don't dare raise questions about the administration. They think that if they did that they'd lose their jobs. For most of them, that isn't true at all. Most of them could get by, could do much more than they realize they can do. Their limits are not as tight, not as close to them as they think. So I'm always suggesting to people that they test out how far they can push those limits and do it in a quiet sort of a way, kind of a pilot project to see how far they can go. I think most people will find out they can go much further in an institution that is big and bureaucratic and depends primarily on reports and grades. Administrators don't look into the classroom so long as things seem to fit. So I think there's a lot more leeway in every field. At Highlander, sometimes we're a little too cautious and we don't push the boundaries far enough. We could go further.

Now I've been criticized for advocating that people push their boundaries because sometimes people get caught. Sometimes people get fired. Sometimes people lose their jobs because of pushing the boundaries too far, but it's an interesting experience. They found they didn't want to stay within those limitations that they were pushing. Once people find they can survive outside the limits, they're much happier. They don't want to feel trapped. So I think we can urge people to push the boundaries as far as they can, and if they get in trouble, fine; that's not too bad if that's what they want to do.

CHAPTER 4

Educational Practice

"The more the people become themselves, the better the democracy"

PAULO: Education always implies program, content, method, objectives and so on, as I said yesterday. For me it has always been a political question, not exclusively an educational question, at what levels students take part in the process of organizing the curriculum. I know that this question has to have different answers according to different places and times. The more people participate in the process of their own education, the more the people participate in the process of defining what kind of production to produce, and for what and why, the more the people participate in the development of their selves. The more the people become themselves, the better the democracy. The less people are asked about what they want, about their expectations, the less democracy we have.

MYLES: I use questions more than I do anything else. They don't think of a question as intervening because they don't realize that the reason you asked that question is because you know something. What you know is the body of the material that you're trying to get people to consider, but instead of giving a lecture on it, you ask a question enlightened by that. Instead of you getting on a pinnacle you put them on a pinnacle. I think there's a lot of confusion in the minds of academicians as to what you mean when you say you have to intervene.

PAULO: Yeah, it's very good that you said this because I use intervention exactly in the way you use it.

MYLES: Yes, I know you do, but you'd better try to explain it a little better, because other people will misunderstand you.

THIRD PARTY: Myles, in those early days, how did you see your role? How did you evolve your technique of intervention? What did you do?

MYLES: Well, I take the same position as Paulo, that you have the responsibility, if you have some knowledge or some insight, to share that with people. If you have a conviction, you have a responsibility to act on that conviction where you can, and if you're doing education, you act on it in an educational context.

I reacted to the way I was educated, which I thought was miseducation. I thought there ought to be a better way. I've always resented being put down by teachers showing their knowledge and presuming that I didn't have any. The truth about the matter was that I was in situations like this when I was in school in Brazil [Tenn.], where I knew more than the teacher, and I knew I knew more than the teacher. I started experimenting with ways to get my ideas across without putting people down, with trying to get them to think and analyze their own experiences. So I rediscovered what's long been known, that one of the best ways to educate is to ask questions. Nothing new about that. It's just not widely practiced in academic life. I guess the academicians give you a lecture on it, but they couldn't practice it. So I just found that if I know something well enough, then I can find a way in the discussion that's going on to inject that question at the right time, to get people to consider it. If they want to follow it up, then you ask more questions, growing out of that situation. You can get all your ideas across just by asking questions and at the same time you help people to grow and not form a dependency on you. To me it's just a more successful way of getting ideas across.

THIRD PARTY: Then it becomes their idea.

MYLES: It becomes theirs because they're the ones who come to that idea, not because I said it or because of some authority; it just makes sense. It makes sense because it's related to the process and the thinking they're going through.

THIRD PARTY: It's kind of subversive isn't it?

MYLES: Well yes, I guess, if you say being subversive is that you try to get your ideas across. I've never hesitated to tell anybody what I believe about anything if they ask me. I see no reason to tell them before they get ready to listen to it, and when they ask a question, then they're ready to listen to it. I just don't see any point in wasting your energy trying to force something on people. We have a saying here. You probably have similar sayings in your culture in Brazil. We say you can lead a horse to water but you can't make him drink.

PAULO: Yes.

MYLES: This is a problem they deal with in academia by hitting the horse over the head and beating on him till they force his nose in the tub, and just to keep the blows from continuing, he'll try to drink. My system is to make him thirsty, so he'll volunteer to drink.

PAULO: Yes.

THIRD PARTY: But, Myles, did it take you some practice to get to the point so you always knew how to handle those questions?

MYLES: Oh, did it!

THIRD PARTY: Let's talk about that a little bit.

MYLES: See, when I tell something like this, you think I'm saying I was born with a gray beard, like I was born like I am now.

THIRD PARTY: It is confusing because you also said you didn't believe in experimenting on people.

MYLES: Not *on* people but with people. You experiment with people not on people. There's a big difference. They're in on the experiment. They're in on the process. At what point do you get good at something? I had a reputation for being good at leading discussions, but I didn't have that reputation in the first years of the school, when we were trying to figure out how to use our academic knowledge on people.

For example, we always had the practice at Highlander, back when I was director, of having the staff acquainted with the area in which we were working. There were two ways. We would respond to a student's request for help or we'd just roam around the region to find out what was going on. We needed to know what was happening in the economic, social, and cultural realm where we were working, but we didn't come in and make a lecture on it or write a book about it. We used this knowledge to have insights out of which we asked questions and led discussions. So you had to be knowledgeable; you had to know your subject. You had to know more than the people that you were teaching or you wouldn't have anything to contribute. You didn't have to know more about where they were in their development. They knew more about that than you did. You didn't have to know more about their experiences. They were the world's authority on their own experience and you need to value that, appreciate that.

Highlander has a videotape of a workshop in which Mike Clark, the director at that time, asks one question, and that one question turned that workshop around and completely moved it in a different direction. Well, that was one short question, but Mike had years of experience in the region, out of which he asked that question. Now that's what I mean by using your content. Use your familiarity with your subject, but use it as a basis. First it's a matter of conviction that that's the way you should deal with people, that you should respect them and let them develop their own thinking without you trying to think for them. But how do you do that? You have to practice till you find out you know how to do it, and then it's like anything else. Like a musician just learning, sit down at the piano and start playing. You just start doing it. It's natural. You don't have to give it a great deal of thought. You just intuitively say, "Well, what can I do here?" And it kind of comes out, but that's practice. That's practice.

PAULO: Concerning this question of not respecting the knowledge, the common sense of the people. Last week I was in Recife leading a seminar for a group of educators, and we were discussing precisely this question of respecting knowledge of the people. A teacher told us a very interesting story. She said that academic learning, the fact of being an academic, is not bad. It's just what *kind* of academic. A student went to a fishing area to do some research, and he met a fisherman who was coming back from fishing. The academic asked, "Do you know who is the president of the country?" The fisherman said, "No, I don't know." "Do you know the name of the governor of the state?" He said, "I'm afraid that I don't know." And then the academic, losing patience, said, "But at least you know the name of the local authority." The fisherman said, "No I also don't know, but taking advantage of asking these questions about names of people, I would like to ask you: Do you know the name of this fish?" And the academic said no. "But, that one you know, don't you?" The academic said no. "But this third one, you have to know," and the academic said, "No, I also don't know." The fisherman said, "Do you see? Each one with his ignorance."

MYLES: There's a mountain story, same plot but different story, of a traveling salesman here in the mountains. He

got lost and he didn't know which way to go. He found
a little boy beside the road, and he said, "Hey there son,
do you know the way to Knoxville?" The boy said, "No,
sir." And he said, "Do you know the way to Gatlinburg?"
"No, sir." Well, he said, "Do you know the way to Sevier-
ville?" The boy said, "No, sir." And he said, "Boy, you
don't know much, do you?" "No, sir, but I ain't lost!"

THIRD PARTY: It seems to me that you keep coming back in
the conversations again and again to this point of the
delicate relationship between teaching, giving knowledge, and learning knowledge. Paulo talks about going
beyond the knowledge that the people bring. Now I sus-
pect that you do that too. Paulo articulates going beyond the knowledge of the people, and Myles articulates beginning with the knowledge of the people, so
somewhere in between there there's a practice that both
of you have.

MYLES: I have a personal philosophy of what I think the
world should be like, what life should be like. Now as I
said yesterday I have no rights that shouldn't be made
universal, and if I can understand this has any validity
and authenticity, then other people can understand it. I
start with that premise, so now the question is how you
expose people, move people on to where they'll take a
look at this. That's the whole purpose of what I perceive
Highlander to be. You stay within the experience of
the people, and the experience is growing right there,
in what I call a circle of learners, in a workshop situation. They're growing because they've learned from
their peers. They've learned not what they knew but
knew they didn't know. They learned something from

the questions you've raised. You've got them to thinking, so right there before your eyes their experience is
changing. You're not talking about the experience they
brought with them. You're talking about the experience
that is given them in the workshop, and in a few days
time that experience can expand termendously. But if
you break the connection between the starting point,
their experience, and what they know themselves, if
you get to the place where what they know can't help
them understand what you're talking about, then you
lose them. Then you reach the outside limits of the
possibility of having any relationship to those people's
learning. So you have to be very careful in analyzing a
group to know that they're ready to talk about ancient
Greece, if that throws light on the subject, or if they're
ready to talk about what's happening in Patalonia or
Brazil, what's happened in the Soviet Union. Information that brings those things out may be a movie or may
be a discussion, because it's still part of their experience. Their experience is not only what they came with.
If it only stays there, there's no use to start.

Now my experience has been that if you do this thing
right, carefully, and don't get beyond participants at
any one step, you can move very fast to expand their
experience very wide in a very short time. But you have
to always remember, if you break that connection, it's
no longer available to their experience, then they don't
understand it, and it won't be useful to them. Then it
becomes listening to the expert tell them what to do,
and they'll go back home and try to do it without under-

standing it or even thinking they need to understand it, you see. That's no good.

I never feel limited by this process at all. I feel liberated by it. I feel I can raise questions that are much more far-reaching and much more in-depth and much more radical, much more revolutionary, this way than I could if I was talking to them and trying to explain things to them. I use it as a way to get in more, not less. I don't feel like I'm riding roughshod over people by trying to get them to share my ideas. I don't have any guilt problems about this at all. I think it's my responsibility to share what I believe in, not only in discussions but in the way I live and in the way the workshops run and in the way Highlander's run, the way life is.

Rosa Parks talks about her experience at Highlander, and she doesn't say a thing about anything *factually* that she learned. She doesn't say a thing about any subject that was discussed. She doesn't say a thing about integration. She says the reason Highlander meant something to her and emboldened her to act as she did was that at Highlander she found *respect* as a black person and found white people she could *trust*. So you speak not just by words and discussion but you speak by the way your programs are run. If you believe in something, then you have to practice it. People used to come to Highlander when there were very few places, if any, in the South where social equality was accepted. We shared it by doing it and not by talking about it. We didn't have to make a speech about it. We didn't even have to ask questions about it. We did it. So, it's all tied together, doing everything you can to share your ideas. There's no such thing as just being a coordinator or facilitator, as if you don't know anything. What the hell are you around for, if you don't know anything. Just get out of the way and let somebody have the space that knows something, believes something.

THIRD PARTY: Are there specific examples in particular of that delicate balance between *bringing out* the knowledge of the people and *going beyond* their knowledge, as Paulo puts it, and how this is reflected in practice? Theoretically, that is something that people understand, but in day-to-day practice, it's very often hard to really come to terms with and to know exactly how to do it.

MYLES: It's quite obvious that you can't transfer an institution, like it was obvious to me that you couldn't take a Danish folk school and plunk it down in the mountains of east Tennessee any more than you could take a Danish beech tree and cut it off at the top of the ground and stand it up on the ground in the United States and have it grow. When you get down to this transferring level, helping somebody jump from one understanding to another, then it gets rather ticklish as to what the difference is between helping people grow in understanding and unfolding what's already there. There comes a point when you've got to ask if this idea really fits. Will this idea aid this process of growth? This is a problem that has always bothered me, exactly how far you could go in stretching people's experience without breaking the thread. In radical education, people who claim to

be Freirians to my mind make a lot of mistakes, making
assumptions about people's experience and knowledge.

PAULO: I think that this is one of the main points of which
radical educators have to be aware. If someone is an
educator, it means then that this person is involved with
a process or some kind of action with others who are
named the students. This educator can be working, for
example, inside of the school and he or she has system-
atized practice. He or she has a certain curriculum to
follow, and he or she teaches a particular content to the
students. It is the same for an educator who works out
of the school, out of the subsystem of education. For
example, an educator at Highlander does not have necessarily a curriculum, in the broader meaning of this.
The Highlander educator does not have necessarily a
list of subjects to talk about, to explain to students.
Nevertheless, there is something that for me is impossible, and that is the absence of some content about
which they speak. What must be the central difference
is that in Highlander's experience, the contents come
up from analysis, from the thinking of those who are
involved in the process of education—that is, not exclusively from the educator who chooses what he or she
thinks to be the best, for the students, but also those who
come to participate. It is as if they were suddenly in a
circle, like this house,* getting some distance from their

* The central meeting room at Highlander is circular in shape. Rock-
ing chairs, a fireplace, and a spectacular view of the Smoky Mountains
provide a comfortable atmosphere for workshops.

155

experience in order to understand the reasons why they are having this kind of experience. It means that also in this setting, the educator, even though he or she is different from a public-school educator, does not transfer knowledge to the group of people who come here. As far as I understand Myles's thinking and practice, with his team here, I see that in all the fundamental moments of Highlander's history—in the thirties, in the fifties, in the sixties, in the seventies, in every moment—the educators here have been educators but have accepted *to be educated* too. That is, they understood, even though they did not read Marx, what Marx meant when he said that "the educator himself must be educated."

MYLES: Yes. Bernice Robinson, the first Citizenship School teacher, says that the most important thing she did was to say the first time the people got together: "Now I'm *not* a school teacher. I'm here to learn with you." Now she didn't get that from Marx. She got that as a black woman from her experience.

PAULO: But what is fantastic, Myles, in the history of this experience is that in learning with those who come here, you also taught them, that it should be possible for educators just to learn with the students. Both are engaged in the process in which both grew up. Educators have some systematic knowledge that the students necessarily don't have yet. . . . And now I think that I am coming near the question.

THIRD PARTY: Sneaking up on it.

PAULO: Yes, this is my way of working, of thinking. First I try to make a circle so the issue can't escape.

When the students come, of course, they bring with

them, inside of them, in their bodies, in their lives, they bring their hopes, despair, expectations, knowledge, which they got by living, by fighting, by becoming frustrated. Undoubtedly they don't come here empty. They arrive here full of things. In most of the cases, they bring with them opinions about the world, about life. They bring with them their knowledge at the level of common sense, and they have the right to go beyond this level of knowledge. At the same time—I want to be very clear, in order to avoid being understood as falling into a certain scientificism—there are levels of knowledge about the facts they already know, which unveil other ways of knowing, which can give us much more exact knowledge about the facts. This is a right that the people have, and I call it the right to know better what they already know. Knowing better means precisely going beyond the *common sense* in order to begin to discover the *reason* for the facts.

Right now I can tell a small story. One month ago I was talking at home with one of my friends, one of the directors of the working class institute I spoke about earlier. At the end of a course about workers' lives, a young man said, "When I came here I was sure that I already knew many many things about these issues, but I was not as clear about the *reasons* for them as I am now." What this young worker meant is precisely the central question you asked. That is, how, starting from where people are, to go with them beyond these levels of knowledge without just *transferring* the knowledge. The question is not to come to the classroom and to make beautiful speeches analyzing, for example, the political authority of the country, but the question is how to take advantage of the reading of reality, which the people are doing, in order to make it possible for students to make a different and much *deeper* reading of reality.

The question is not to impose readings on students, no matter that they are university students, but how to put together critically, dialectically, the reading of the texts in relationship to the contexts, and the understanding of the contexts that can be helped through the reading of texts. This also is the question, how to make this walk with people starting from more or less naive understanding of reality. Starting from people's experiences, and not from *our* understanding of the world, does not mean that we don't want the people to come with us in order to go beyond us afterward. This movement for me is one of the many important roles of a progressive educator, and it is not always so easy.

I think that we have to create in ourselves, through critical analysis of our practice, some qualities, some virtues as educators. One of them, for example, is the quality of becoming more and more open to feel the feelings of others, to become so sensitive that we can guess what the group or one person is thinking at that moment. These things cannot be taught as content. These things have to be learned through the example of the good teacher.

MYLES: This is a problem, how we can have a body of knowledge and understanding and resist the temptation to misread the interest of the people because we're look-

ing for an opportunity to unload this great load of gold
that we have stored up.

PAULO: Not to do that, Myles, is one of the other virtues.

MYLES: Now that blinds us sometimes, it seems to me, from
observing the action of the people, the nonverbal language, because we are thinking verbally, and we're only
looking for verbal reactions and we don't read anything else.

PAULO: The bodies.

MYLES: We don't want to see that because it wouldn't encour-
age us to agree that they are with us. Now that's a real
problem that I have to struggle with. I've observed that
I have two roles, one as a what you might call an educator in relation to the situation and one as a person who
has subjective experience I'd like to share with people,
knowledge that I've picked up one way or another. I've
got to keep those two things separate, but in my enthu-
siasm, sometimes I mix the two.

One of the things I've found is that if any one of a
group of people with similar problems asks a question,
then there's a good chance that the question will reflect
some of the thinking of the peers. Even if it doesn't,
everybody in that circle is going to listen to the answer
to that question, because one of their peers asked it.
They can identify with the questioner. It's a *clue* that
there's some interest there. Short of questions, I have
found that I'm secure in a discussion when people actually say what they perceive a situation to be. Then I
know where I am. But there's always gradations, from
the certainty up to the guessing, the temptation to guess

in favor of your subjectivity, *your* experience instead of *their* experience. How do you deal with that?

PAULO: Yes. There is another obstacle for such an attitude vis-à-vis the object of knowledge and vis-à-vis the students as cognitive subjects, which is the dominant ideology introjected by the students no matter whether they are workers or students of the university. That is, they come absolutely convinced that the teacher has to *give* a class to them.

MYLES: They have the answers.

PAULO: Do you see? They come just to receive answers for any questions they asked before. As you said, this is an obstacle—how to confront a group of students who, in perceiving that you are interested in knowing what they know, think that you are not capable. Is it clear that the students . . .

MYLES: . . . View you as an authority figure.

PAULO: Yes. They expect you to give the first class in an old style, and you say no, I would like first of all to talk a little bit about the very content we should study this semester. And then one of the students can say to himself or herself, this professor is not capable, above all if the professor is a young person. Several graduate students in São Paulo told me how they were obliged to start immediately, giving a list of books and speaking a lot, because the students felt insecure. I think that in such a case, the teacher, understanding the situation, should be 50 percent a traditional teacher and 50 percent a democratic teacher in order to begin to challenge the students, and for them to change a little bit too.

With regard to popular groups, I think if they did

not have too much experience in the school system, the situation is a little bit different. Of course they can be frightened because they think that the educator is a so-called intellectual and they don't see themselves also as intellectuals. They cannot understand that. They think that they don't have culture because the cultured man or woman has first to come to university. Then it's necessary to exercise this discipline you talked about, the discipline of controlling a second intellectual taste that we intellectuals always have, which is speaking about what we think that we know. In the works by Amilcar Cabral there is something very interesting that sometimes shows up very clearly, which is the dialecticity between patience and impatience. Based on Amilcar I always say that, in effect, we should work "impatiently patient." There is a moment when we can go a little farther and say something, and there is a moment in which we should listen more to the people.

MYLES: Yes. Sometimes I think of it in terms of a figure. You try to stretch people's minds and their understanding, but if you move too fast then you break the connection. You go off and leave them, and so they aren't being stretched in their thinking. In popular education, my experience is that working and poor people all come with an expectation. Since they've been told they can learn something, and what they're to learn is the answers to their problems, they expect an expert with answers. Even if they haven't been in school in a long time, they're socialized by society to look for an expert. So I start out by acknowledging that that's why they've come. Then I say, you know you have a lot of problems. And I just use that as a jumping off place, so to speak, to ask them to talk about their experience. Let's see what's in your experience and not in the experience of experts.

You set the stage for doing something that they're uncomfortable with. You know they're uncomfortable with it, and you have to work through that business of getting them to be comfortable with trusting themselves a little bit, trusting their peers a little bit. They hear Mary say something and Susie says well, if they listen to Mary, maybe they'll listen to me. It's a slow process, but once the people get comfortable with it, then they begin to see that you aren't going to play the role of an expert, except in the sense that you are the expert in *how* they're going to learn, not in *what* they're going to learn. It's a slow and tedious process but it seems to work.

Now I'll admit at times in situations I've had to do what you said, Paulo, do part of the old and part of the new. I remember one time here in Tennessee, I was trying to help a group of farmers get organized into a cooperative, and they announced that I was coming to speak at this country schoolhouse. Well, I knew their expectation was that I would speak as an expert. I knew if I didn't speak, and said "let's have a discussion about this," they'd say that guy doesn't know anything. So I said, what I have to do is make a speech because I don't want to lose the interest they've built up, and I can't change them instantaneously. So I made a speech, the best speech I could. Then after it was over, while we were still there, I said, let's discuss this speech. Let's discuss what I have said. Well now, that was just one step removed, but close enough to their expectation that I was able to carry them along. So the discussion ended without resolving a lot of problems that I had raised. They were analyzing what I had said. I couldn't get them to talk about their *own* experiences because they were still looking to the experts. Before I left I said, now it'd be good if we could talk about *your* experience. We've talked about my experience, now let's talk about yours. Could we come back next week? And you will be the speakers. In this way I was able to get started with them. I never had to make another speech. You do have to make concessions like that.

"Highlander is a weaving of many colors"

THIRD PARTY: Myles, I'd like some more examples of what Paulo's talking about in terms of the practice with popular education. I know with the labor schools, for instance, at Highlander that you would do classes on parliamentary procedure and how to put out a newsletter and very specific things that I know grew out of requests. With the civil rights movement, it was different. Would you talk about how you got to those two different places. Or maybe they're not different places at all. How did you determine what to do in working with the labor movement? And then how was it different with the civil rights movement, if it was.

MYLES: No, the labor period was the first experience we'd actually had in a structured sort of program. We had to start with what they perceived their problems to be. Our job was to develop local leadership for the new industrial unions and to help the new local union officers understand better how to function. That was what they wanted. Now what we wanted in addition to that was to help them understand that they should work with a larger community. They should work with farmers, they should deal with integration, they should be part of the world. We had our own agenda.

Now in form we tried as far as possible to do it the way they would expect us to do, because it was relevant to solving their problems. In the way Highlander was run, we would do what we thought was important. Two things just right off hand: One was that Highlander's integrated, so we didn't have to talk about that problem, we did it. And two, we based our whole thinking on the premise that people learn what they do. Not what they talk about but what they do. And so we made our speech about social equality without saying anything, but by *doing* it.

We also believed that they had to be good officials of the unions and that a lot of them would be organizers. They had to learn to think, make decisions—not learn gimmicks, not learn techniques, but learn how to *think*. So in an effort to help them understand the importance of learning how to think, we had them, with no strings attached, in full control of the week or two weeks they were there. They made every decision about everything: classes, teachers, visitors, subject matter. They resisted that with everything they had because they had never had an opportunity to make decisions in a "school," and they thought that was our responsibility. Now I dealt with that by having each group, at the end of the session, say here is what we have learned here, and here is what we propose the *next* group do. We think we can share our learning with them and this is what we proposed that they do. That was done every session. When a new group came, I would say, this is what the last group proposed you do. Now since you haven't had any experience in making decisions about these things, it's all new to you. The first day let's start by doing what people like you thought would be good. After the first day, in the evening, we will organize for the week or two weeks. We'll set up committees—because we try to get them used to using committees in unions—on public relations, on discipline, on subject matter, on visiting speakers, on relations with the community, on running a co-op, because we were trying to get them to understand the economic element in addition to unions. So we turned it all over to them, and they were in complete control. I mean they *exercised* that control. The program was recognizable to them in terms of what they had been told and it was similar enough to schooling that it didn't seem too unfamiliar. You've gotta have a structure that participants can feel comfortable with until they begin to have something to deviate from or add to. Now what they really do would not change things very much from session to session. The schedule was made by people like themselves, and they recognized it as authentic. They would make a few adaptations and changes as they went along.

We had somebody come to teach about the labor board [National Labor Relations Board] who gave a lot of things to read. The students said: "Hey, wait a minute. We want to discuss this with you. We want to ask you some questions." The visitor said: "It's all in this book. Look it up." The student said: "We don't need you. Just give us the books and go. We don't need you if you don't know what's in them. If we're going to have to read the books, then you go back to Washington, and we'll sit here and read them." That's the way they dealt with visiting speakers. They weren't cowed by anybody, and we were happy about that, because they were beginning to take control of the situation. They'd tell us what to do all the time.

Now, in dealing with grievances, Zilphia was one of the best. She used a lot of drama in teaching how to handle grievances and kept people's interest by role-playing. That was pre-role-playing days, before it had a name, but it was the same thing! The process, the way she worked and the way I worked is one thing we had in common. We not only talked about how to take up a grievance and how to write one, we did it, we played out the whole scene. Students did need to know the technique of how to write up a grievance, if they could write, and they needed to know that they had to have arguments, but we said that won't win a grievance. What wins the grievance is to have a strong group of workers in your department. If you've got the workers with you, then that's the way to get your grievances settled.

Now how are you going to get the workers with you? You've got black people, women, old timers in your plants. We'd go into why you had to involve everybody and why you couldn't discriminate. It takes the power of everyone united to get a grievance settled. So we'd take even settling arguments, which is usually kind of a technical thing, as a basis for educating people about democracy. In everything we did, those elements came out. In a class on union problems, the students would raise problems that they had, and we'd discuss them. And I knew the problems those people had because I'd dealt with the same kinds of people over and over again. I knew more about their problems than they did, but I didn't tell them that. I never, never put down a problem on the blackboard or listed a problem that they didn't list, even though I knew it was their problem, and I didn't do what I see some people doing today. I didn't put it in my own words and revise it to make it clear. I've seen that happen in these training programs, where somebody will say something and then they'll re-write it so it makes more sense. That's a put-down to a worker to edit his or her way of saying things. So the workers worded the problems. First I would ask, "What do you know about that problem already?" Then they said, "I don't know anything." Well okay, you know how to survive, you're here. Your union sent you here. They thought you had some leadership ability. I would push them to name what they know, and they find right off, with a little struggle and a lot of embarrassment, that there are some things that they can articulate. They don't need any games or any playing around. The one thing they know is their own experience. They don't need to homogenize it with other people's experience. They want to talk about their own experience. Then other people join in and say, "Ah ha, I had an experience that relates to that." So pretty soon you get everybody's experiences coming in, centered around that *one* person's experience, because that's an *authentic* experience not a *synthetic* experience. Authentic. And everybody recognizes authenticity. Workers recognize authenticity. Academic people quite often don't *want* authenticity. They want some kind of synthesis that takes the experience a little bit away, so it'll be more bearable to them, I suppose. But they recognize this is authentic.

After everybody had the benefit of hearing everybody else's problem discussed, we would ask on the basis of what you've learned that you knew—that you didn't know before that you knew—and on the basis of your fellow workers' experiences, now how do you think it'll be best to deal with these problems? It was so enriching, you see, to have a person learn that they knew something. Secondly, to learn that their peers knew something, and learn that they didn't have to come to me, the expert, to tell them what the answers were. Then they planned: here's how we'll deal with this problem when we go back home.

Now that was the way the whole labor school was run. We taught a lot of things that they needed to know. They needed to make speeches. They needed parliamentary law, which I don't believe in, but they needed it. But they also needed, we thought, a lot of other things. We tried to involve everybody in singing and doing drama and dancing and laughing and telling stories, because that's a part of their life. It's more of a holistic approach to education, not just a bunch of unrelated segments. The way people live was more important than any class or any subject that we were dealing with. That's an extremely important experience. They had that learning experience, making decisions, living in an unsegregated fashion, enjoying their senses other than their minds. It was that experience that was probably worth more than any *factual* things that they learned, although you know there were some factual things that they learned.

This didn't mean that we didn't add to that mix. Once you get people talking about a problem and there's no solution within the group, which is often the case, then you go outside the group and introduce ideas and experiences that are related to the problem. Workers in other places, in other countries, and in other ages, all are relevant if they're related to the problems at hand. People's minds get opened up to wanting to know all these things. They'll ask questions. How did the labor movement get started in England? What caused the revolution in Russia? Why do people call us communists when we organize? I remember one time I said just go to the encyclopedia and read about what communism is, and they said, is it in the encyclopedia? They thought it was something the manufacturing association had cooked up! They read the definition and they discussed that. They took an "encyclopedia class," but that was an extension of that experience. I didn't say, now you need to know what communism is. If I'd said that, they wouldn't have ever bothered to read it.

We can use current examples. The Bumpass Cove people, for example, didn't know when they first came here that they could know what toxic chemicals did to people. They thought that that's something they had to go to the health officials and the company officials for. Even though they knew the officials were lying to them, it didn't occur to them that there was any way for them to find out for themselves. When they asked what are these chemicals, Juliet Merrifield, who was working with them, said well, let's go down to the library and look it up—just like I said look up communism. They ended up, as they say in the movie, making their own list.* They didn't know they could know that when they started out, because they'd been denied the opportunity to know that they could know about chemicals and their effects. They thought that was in the realm of experts.

PAULO: Listening to Myles, I felt challenged to make some reflections about one of the points.

MYLES: Good. That's what I wanted you to do.

PAULO: Of course I am in agreement with this global vision you give us. The first reflection, which is good to under-line, is how *difficult* is the task of an educator. No matter where this kind of educator works, the great difficulty— or the great adventure!—is how to make education something which, in being serious, rigorous, methodi-cal, and having a process, also creates happiness and joy.

MYLES: Joy. Yes—happiness, joy.

PAULO: That difficulty is how to give an example to the stu-dents that in working on the practice, on the personal experience, we necessarily go beyond what we did. For

---

* Lucy Massie Phenix, producer, *You Got to Move: Stories of Change in the South* (New York: Icarus Films, 1985).

example, if I know critically what I did in planting seeds, if I know what I did during the act of planting, if I get the reason *why*, of course I go beyond what I did. I had a kind of umbrella, a framework of knowledge, which was not so clear at that point. Beginning with what I learned initially, I discovered lots of possible extensions of knowledge, which were otherwise almost invisible.

Then coming back to the question of joy, of seriousness. I am afraid, Myles—maybe I am not humble in saying that I am sure that you agree with me—that one of the risks we have as educators is to think that the practice of educating, of teaching, should be reduced just into joy. Happiness. And then the educator would not to have any kind of demand on the students, would not make any kind of suggestion to the students to be more rigorous in studying, because the teacher cannot cut off the students' right to be happy. This transforms the practice of education into a kind of entertainment. The other risk is to be so serious that seriousness fights against happiness. Then instead of having a childlike practice, you have a very rigid face of an old and despairing figure! Does it make sense? Don't teach like this; but a great many educators do.

For example, for me it is difficult to *begin* studying. Studying is not a free task. It's not a gift. Studying is demanding, hard, difficult. But inside of the difficulty, happiness begins to be generated. At some point suddenly we become absolutely happy with the results, which come from having been serious and rigorous. Then for me one of the problems that we have as educators in our line is how never, never to lose this complexity of our action and how never to lose even one of the ingredients of the practice. I cannot understand a school that makes children sad about going to school. This school is bad. But I also don't accept a school in which the kids spend all the time just playing. This school is also bad. The good school is that one in which in studying I also get the pleasure of playing. I learn how to have intellectual discipline. Look, being disciplined, democratically, is something that takes part of life. It's vital for me to have some intellectual discipline in order to get knowledge, in order to know better.

Then there is another point about which I would like to make a comment. Myles said something very important when he stressed the question of thinking. It's absolutely necessary to teach how to think critically, but—I don't know whether Myles agrees with me—it's impossible for me in this kind of education to teach *how* to think unless we are teaching something, some content to the students. I want to say that it's impossible to teach how to think by just thinking. That is, I have to teach how to think, thinking about something and then knowing something. But this is precisely what this Highlander Center has done for the past fifty years. Myles told us about asking people, If the advice of the experts worked in the past, why then are you here now? If you are here now because you were not satisfied with the results of the other way of working, why didn't we pick this way? Why not walk another road? When Myles asked this, undoubtedly they were very enveloped by his questions and his speech—not just thought, but action. There was some content in that. He was just awakening their memories concerning some knowledge and concrete experiences. The *content* was there, but not so easily seen sometimes. Because of that, it was possible to challenge the group to think in a different way and also to understand the need for getting a new road. The acceptance of doing something different has to do with the understanding of a former experience in which there were subjects that were discussed. What Myles did was to touch their memory about a subject and to remake the road.

I think that it's really impossible to teach how to think more critically by just making a speech about critical thought. It's absolutely indispensable to give a witness, an example, of thinking critically to the students. This is the reason why the experience here has been so good. You always had here a subject that you discussed together with the people, and in satisfying some of the students' needs, necessarily the people went beyond the subject matter.

MYLES: We've always done these things imperfectly. Always.

PAULO: All of us work imperfectly.

MYLES: Always. I don't think I ever did a workshop in which I didn't think later, my goodness I should've known better than to do this. Or, if I had just thought fast enough, I could've helped people understand this from their experience. To this day, I never have the satisfaction of saying this is a perfect job, well done. I've learned something in this job, I hope I can do better next time, but I just have to keep on learning different things.

I would say, just parenthetically, I started out back when I was more book oriented teaching a course on how to think! Somebody had a little book on how to think, and I thought the way to go about teaching people how to think was to teach them what was in the book.

THIRD PARTY: You taught this at Highlander?

MYLES: Yes! The first year. That's when we were really learning. From then on I didn't find the book too helpful, certainly, to use as text. I used the text from the people's experiences after that. But I remember very well starting that way, not knowing that these people didn't have to learn the same way schooling taught people. I wouldn't have known then, to use an example that we talked about, that the people who came here looking for experts really had the answer to that problem through their experience. We've all come a long ways in this, and of course there's a long ways to go.

THIRD PARTY: When you were talking about not ever doing anything perfectly, it seems to me that some of the best learning that I had here as a staff member was in reflecting on a workshop after we had done it, about what we had done right and about what we had done wrong. I wanted to hear you talk some about your own growth as an educator with your peer educators at Highlander and how that process developed over the years.

MYLES: Well see, we all started out with similar academic backgrounds. We were all philosophically socialists, so we had similar goals. So we had to learn together, and I don't mean it wasn't uneven. Some people learned faster or better than others, and some learned something that somebody else didn't learn, but we were peers and so it was easy to communicate. We did some evaluations like you're talking about. If you look at the old records, as you probably have, you'll see all kinds of long analyses of what we were doing, what we believed in, what was going wrong. We spent a lot of time being very critical, and we invited criticism from the outside. We were trying to get all the help we could in thinking through the problems because we had a very definite sense that we didn't know what we were doing. We were really embarrassed by our inefficiency, to the place where we were struggling. When we invited criticism we got it. I remember that somebody said that I was cruel. I was dealing with a group of young people, and one of the girls cried because she said I made her very unhappy and that I should make people happy, not suffer. I said, well, these were teenagers. When they grow physically they have joy and pain. They have aches, actually. Growing is a painful process, but they have joy in being young. I mean what I'm doing with the mind is the same as nature does with the body. It's no different. I think you should stretch people to their limits and our limits. But those kinds of criticisms would come up.

Then there were criticisms from the left, that we weren't making enough speeches telling people what to believe, and we didn't have the right belief ourselves. And from the right, saying we were revolutionaries, that we were subverting the system. Someone criticized us for getting money from capitalists and fighting capitalism, saying you're biting the hand that feeds you. I said, who else can feed us? In a capitalist society there's no other place for money to come from. Money has to come from the system, and people that we identify with produce that wealth. We get the money where the money is and use it where the people are. The critic said, but don't you feel awkward about biting the hand that feeds you? I said no, I enjoy just gnawing it up to the shoulder. That was on a public TV program. It haunted me for years, the image of a one-armed capitalist!

We had all kinds of problems we had to deal with, and that was part of education. We weren't just in the mechanics of education. That was never much of a feature at Highlander. We've talked more about it here than we did for years. We just did it. I came out with a strong conviction that nothing, no methodology or no technique was as near as important as the way I did things myself, in terms of my teaching other people. If I stopped having joy in learning, I could no longer help give anybody else joy in learning.

PAULO: Yes, of course.

MYLES: And you know what you do has to be compatible. If I believe in social equality and don't practice it, then what I say is hollow. You have to have that kind of consistency. That's why I'm less interested in methodology or techniques than I am in a *process* that involves the total person, involves vision, involves total realities. I think of my grandfather, who was an illiterate mountaineer and who had a good mind, although he couldn't write his name. He used to say, "Son you're talking about all these ideas, and you got your wagon hitched to a star, but you can't haul anything in it that's not down on earth." I know you have to have it hitched to the star, and he did too, but it's also got to be down on earth where something practical can be done. You have to tie the practical with the visionary.

I think if I had to put a finger on what I consider a good education, a good *radical* education, it wouldn't be anything about methods or techniques. It would be loving people first. If you don't do that, Ché Guevara says, there's no point in being a revolutionary. I agree with that. And that means all people everywhere, not just your family or your own countrymen or your own color. And wanting for them what you want for yourself. And then next is respect for people's abilities to learn and to act and to shape their own lives. You have to have confidence that people can do that. Now people question me on that. They say, how do you know that? Well, I've had some good experiences. I've gone through two social movements, the industrial union movement and the civil rights movement. I know people can know because I know people can do things, and I know people can die for what they believe in. I know that once people get involved they're willing to do anything they believe is right. I'm not *theorizing* about that, and I'm more fortunate than most people—I think because a lot of people don't know those things like I do, having lived through it and been a part of it. I think our job is to try to figure out ways to help people take over their own lives.

The third thing grows out of caring for people and having respect for people's ability to do things, and that is that you value their experiences. You can't *say* you re-

spect people and not respect their experiences. These
are the kind of elements that seem to me to be important, rather than methodology or techniques. Highlander's a good example of it as an educational entity.
It is hard to talk about Highlander. Highlander can't be
described as an organization because it isn't departmen-
talized and mechanistically conceived. It's more of an
organism, therefore it's hard to describe. It's a mosaic
or a piece of weaving. Back in 1932, if you used colors,
it would be a certain type of color that dominated. Later
on, another color came in and merged with that, and
as Highlander changes the series of colors changes, but
always some of the old and always some of the new.
There's never anything lost. Now two colors may be
blended, and always hopefully something new is intro-
duced, so the weaving is still being made. Highlander
is a kind of a weaving of many colors, some blend and
some clash, but you know it's alive. People during one
historical period *know* that period. We knew the Depression period when we started Highlander. We knew
both the students and activists. We were all student
leaders and activists before we started Highlander, so
we brought that into the beginnings of Highlander.
Later on the civil rights movement came along, and that
came into Highlander and colored a lot of things. We
deliberately set out to be involved in civil rights, and
that brought changes in the process. It actually changed
the composition of the staff. We had more black people.
It changed the composition of the board. Movements
change what goes on and how things are organized.

Later on we had these dull periods, what I call the

organizational period, like we're in now, and we had that kind of "me" period, where people thought that consciousness was limited to their own conscious, something inside themselves. I guess some people thought it would start there and spread to society, but most of it kind of dead-ended there, as far as I could find out. If it starts there it stays there.

You have to have people at Highlander who come out of those periods, to bring in new ways of doing things. We want and welcome new ways of doing things.

Another thing that we started out talking about during the very first pre-Highlander days was that we would be international. We were part of the world but we had to start locally. That has been coming in and out of Highlander's history all along, and now it's playing a bigger role because Highlander's much more Third World–conscious. We think of ourselves as being part of a Third World. Helen Lewis* says that the places we're working are in the peripheries within the periphery. They're the Third Worlds within the Third World, the neglected area. That concept has tied us in with people all over the world. That's one of the colors that has always run through our tapestry. Sometimes it gets bold and sometimes it fades out. Now it's important. The people who come into Highlander bring new insights, but there's still a part of the old, still part of the same piece of tapestry.

---

* Helen Matthews Lewis, Linda Johnson, and Donald Askins, *Colonialism in Modern America: The Appalachian Case* (Boone, N.C.: Appalachian Consortium Press, 1978.)

"Conflicts are the midwife of consciousness"

THIRD PARTY: You mentioned before the concept of responsibility, but at the same time the concept of nonneutrality, political choice. I'm an educator. I am educated by Harvard. At the same time I have a political point of view. The problem is how to how to share, like Myles said, share my point of view without imposing it, without manipulating people. In practical terms it's a very difficult line.

PAULO: I think that this problem is really very important and deserves to be discussed. While having on one hand to respect the expectations and choices of the students, the educator also has the duty of not being neutral, as you said. The educator as an intellectual has to intervene. He cannot be a mere facilitator. He has to affirm to himself or herself. I think that this issue is more or less like the problem of practice and its theory. Do you say that it involves also the question of the authority of the teacher, the freedom of students, the choice of the teacher, the choice of the student, the role the teacher has to teach, the role the teacher has to answer questions, to ask questions, to choose the problems? Sometimes the teacher has the role of leading or the role of speaking, but the teacher has the duty to come from speaking *to* into speaking *with*, for example.

Then for many people, going beyond some risks that we always have in this relationship is something that is not clear. For example, one of the mistakes we can commit in the name of freedom of the students is if I, as a teacher, would paralyze my action and my duty to teach.

In the last analysis, I would leave the students by themselves, and it would be to fall into a kind of irresponsibility. At this moment, afraid of assuming authority, I lose authority. Authority is necessary to the educational process as well as necessary to the freedom of the students and my own. The teacher is absolutely necessary. What is bad, what is *not* necessary, is authoritarianism, but not authority.

If I do that, if I fall with this kind of irresponsibility, instead of generating freedom, I generate license, and then I don't accomplish my responsibility of teaching.

The other mistake is to crush freedom and to exacerbate the authority of the teacher. Then you no longer have freedom but now you have authoritarianism, and then the teacher is the one who teaches. The teacher is the one who knows. The teacher is the one who guides. The teacher is the one who does *everything*. And the students, precisely because the students must be shaped, just expose their bodies and their souls to the hands of the teacher, as if the students were clay for the artist, to be molded. The teacher is of course an artist, but being an artist does not mean that he or she can make the profile, can shape the students. What the educator does in teaching is to make it possible for the students to become themselves. And in doing that, he or she lives the experience of relating democratically as authority with the freedom of the students.

It's the same issue, for example, that we have in the relationship between leadership and masses of the people, between the leadership of a progressive party and the great masses of the people. What is the role of the leadership? It could not be just to *look* at the masses. The role of leadership is also to *lead* the masses while learning with them and never imposing on them. Even I accept that in some moments both teachers and political leaders have to take the initiative in order to do something that is necessary, and it's not possible to wait for tomorrow. But for me, in any case, the next day the teacher as well as the leadership have to begin to explain the reasons why it is necessary to take initiative. In the last analysis, for me it is impossible to take the initiative without explaining why it was necessary.

Because of the importance of this issue, I thought to come back, Myles, to this point in our conversation. As far as I have understood the work of this place, of this institution, respect for communities here does not mean the absence of responsibility on the part of the educators. But we have to recognize that it is not easy. And we also have to assume that the educators have to have initiative.

THIRD PARTY: Myles, can I just add to that one thing. It occurred to me, Paulo, that you always speak of education from the primary level through the university and including the kind of community education that Highlander does. Myles, you speak about adult education for social change, working with people in communities, and I wondered if that makes any difference in the way that you approach this particular issue.

MYLES: Yes I think it does. I think of education as a cradle-to-the-grave education. I use the term *education* in contrast to schooling. I decided before Highlander was started that I wanted to work with adults, and the reasons were that in growing up, commencement speakers always made the same speech that young people are the future leaders of this country. It's up to young people to make this a decent country and solve these problems. And I discovered what everybody else discovered, that they never had any intention of letting the people they were talking to do anything about society. It's a kind of pacification speech. The adults run society. Students don't run society. They have very little to say within the schools let alone society, the larger society. So I decided I wanted to deal with the people who had the power, if they wanted to use it, to change society, because I was interested in changing society. When we started the Highlander Folk School at Monteagle, that thinking was confirmed by a conversation I had with a wonderful woman, May Justus, who was a neighbor and later a board member. She's published fifty-seven children's books. She even had a better record of publication than you have, Paulo! You just have sixteen? She's got fifty-seven! But hers are for children, and they're very thin.

May Justus came to that isolated, mountain community ten years or more before Highlander started. And she would have been a model teacher. She was a mountain woman who came from the neighboring county over here, back in the hills. She had terrific imagination and love for children and love for teaching. She taught my children, Thorsten and Charris. May told me how in grade school, the children were really enthusiastic about life and how she helped them within the confines of the school to have values, to help them love, to have ambition to do something. Then with tears in her eyes, she said the community swallowed them up and they were absorbed into the lethargy of the community, into the hopelessness of the community. They blotted out all that she had been able to get them to understand in school. In other words, she was saying the community is powerful. Adult society is powerful.

I could give dozens and dozens of illustrations, but my point is that I came to the conclusion I wanted to work with the people who, if they chose to—and I was going to try to help them choose—had the power to change society.

Not that I don't appreciate and value other kinds of education, other levels of education. I just chose to work with the people who, historically and practically, are in a position to change society if they choose to so. My idea was to help people choose to change society and to *be with* the people who were in a position to do that. I took this a step further. I wasn't interested in mass education like a schooling system. I was interested in experimenting with ways of working with emerging community leaders or organizational leaders, to try to help those people get a vision and some understanding of how you go about realizing that vision so that they could go back into their communities and spread the ideas. I had never any intention of going into anybody else's community as an expert to solve problems, and then leaving it for those people to follow up. I thought the way to work was to identify people who had a potential for leadership and use that very straightforward simple approach.

I chose to work with organizations that, as far as I

could tell, had a potential, a potential for structural reforms to lead to social movements and to lead to revolutionary change. I was always looking for organizations
that were not aimed at reinforcing the system but aimed
at changing the system insofar as I knew. Now I wasn't
looking for people who were revolutionaries, because I
wouldn't have had anybody to work with. I looked for
people whose organizations had a potential for moving from limited reforms into structural reforms. It
was a very selective group. First I selected adults. Then
within that group, I selected people who had a potential for providing leadership for structural change and
who had a vision of a different future—different from
those who claimed to be neutral and who supported the
status quo.

That was my rationale, and I never faced this di-
chotomy of not being able to share what you had with
people for fear you'd be a propagandist, because my
feeling was that there's no such thing as neutrality. The
people who use that label are people who unknowingly,
for the most part, are dedicated to the support of the
status quo. Now to assume that they do not impose ideas
on people is a proposition I can't accept. They had an
advantage to those of us who want to change society because they are part of society. The people are already in
the society they advocate, in the society they're for, so
they learn by doing the kind of thing that the so-called
neutrals want them to do. We don't have that advantage. I've never felt so powerful that I thought I was
dominating people when I shared my ideas with them.

PAULO: But, Myles, for me that kind of problem is not in

your practice or in mine, but this kind of practical problem really exists for many educators.

MYLES: Yes, I know.

PAULO: Sometimes they are not clear. Some prefer to hide their authoritarian choice with a speech that does not make the problem clear. This is the reason why I found it very interesting that Myles brought this question into the conversation between us. Of course it's not a problem for you and for your educators, but it maybe is a problem for many other people in this country and in Latin America. Some of them may be authoritarian, those who say: "But the experience of Highlander is laissez-faire. It's a kind of living in peace, leaving people by themselves. They are not interfered with." Then it's necessary to discuss this question theoretically.

MYLES: Well, I'm not saying it's not important to discuss. I'm just saying that we understand that the people who claim to be neutral, and call us propagandists because we are not neutral, are not neutral either. They're just ignorant. They don't know that they're supporters of the status quo. They don't know that that's their job. They don't know that the institution is dedicated to perpetuating a system and they're serving an institution. They have influence nevertheless.

PAULO: Many times, Myles, they know really that they are not neutral, but it is necessary for them to insist on neutrality.

THIRD PARTY: I want to go back to the issue of manipulation. You said that there's a clear difference between having authority and authoritarianism. I'm trying to figure out different ways people get the authority they have. Now I want to know what authority you think is legitimate authority.

PAULO: Let's look at that in a very practical way. First of all, let us take a situation at home, in the relationship between the father and the mother and the kids. I am very sure, absolutely sure, that if the father, because he loves his kids, lets them do what they want to do and never shows the kids that there are limits within which we live, create, grow up, then the father does not assume vis-à-vis the kids the responsibility he has to *guide* and to lead. And what is beautiful, I think, philosophically is to see how, apparently starting from outside influence, at some point this discipline begins to start from inside of the kid. That is, this is the road in which we walk, something that comes from outside into autonomy, something that comes from *inside*. That is the result.

It's interesting to see the etymology of education. It means precisely a movement that goes from outside to inside and comes from inside to outside. Then the experience of this movement in life is experience of the relationship between authority and freedom. It is a disaster when father and mother fight against themselves and are not able to give a vision to the kids. I am not saying that the father and the mother never should discuss, because I believe in conflicts. Conflicts are the midwife of consciousness. I am not saying the parents should never fight; they need to fight from time to time. They are not equal and they could not be, but they are not antagonists if they're living together. They are antagonists if they lose love.

187

Now if you go from home into a classroom, it's the same. The nature continues to be the same. That is, the teacher's not the father and the teacher's not the uncle. The teacher is the teacher. He or she has a personality. He's teacher and not uncle and not father or mother, but he has authority. It means that he has some *space* in which he or she has to accomplish some necessary duties from the point of view of the development of the kids. If the teacher does not work like this, if the teacher is too hesitant, if he or she is not competent, if he does or she does not show the students that he has stability and security from an emotional and intellectual point of view, it is difficult to teach. How is it possible to teach without revealing to the students that I am afraid, that I'm insecure. My insecurity destroys my necessary authority with the students. But the other side is how, in assuming the duty of having authority, of living the authority, to balance the necessary authority with the space of freedom of the kids. Then the teacher has to let the kids know that he or she also fights for his or her freedom in another dimension of life—for example, to get a much better salary. The students have to learn with the teacher that teachers also fight in order to free themselves.

For me it is impossible to separate teaching from educating. In educating I teach. In teaching I educate. But sometimes you can see some strange behaviors in which there is apparently a separation between one thing and the other. Maybe a student says to another, remembering school days, "Do you remember Professor Peters?" "Oh yes, I remember. He knew how to give

good classes of mathematics, but no more than that."
You see? It's difficult for students to have a good memory of a teacher who never assumed his or her authority, of a teacher who never established limits.

THIRD PARTY: You speak as if a vision is important in the parent and the teacher. Development of autonomy is part of your vision.

PAULO: Yes.

THIRD PARTY: What if the vision isn't the same? What if the teacher doesn't believe in autonomy for the student or the parent doesn't believe in autonomy? In other words, that's a value that is very important to you and it's very important to Myles. Myles talks about empowering people. He talks about choosing leaders who are going to make a difference. So when you talk about how people have authority, I hear you saying they have to have a vision as very important but I hear more. I hear the vision has to be a specific way. So you're merely saying something very specific about the philosophy of these teachers and these parents?

PAULO: Yes. I insist so much on the clarity of parents and teachers concerning their vision, concerning what they think about the world, about the present, about the future. For me it should take part of the permanent *formation* of the educator. Your question was how to confront and how not to break down the relationship between authority and freedom—that is, how to *share*. There are occasions in which it's almost impossible to share. For example, how is it possible for me to share my vision with a convinced reactionary. I cannot share. But maybe I can share with him or her some *knowledge* about reality, and in doing that maybe I can change him or her from the point of view of my vision.

I don't know whether I am going too far from your question, but it's very interesting to see how it is possible to convert individuals of the ruling class—but never the ruling class as a class. Do you see? It's very interesting. And because of that I think that seminars and workshops like you have had here for over fifty years are such an important source. I can realize, Myles, how many people over these years had the opportunity to become converted as individuals—but as a class, never. For example, Marx; Marx was converted. Fidel Castro was converted. Ché Guevara was converted. I hope that we are being converted.

Because of this, the security of the educator is also important—his or her capacity of loving, of understanding others though without accepting the position of the others, and the ability not to be angry just because you are different. Not to say it's impossible to speak to you because you are different from me. That is, the more secure you are, the clearer your vision, the more you know that you are learning how to put the vision into practice. You know that you are very far from realizing your dream, but if you don't do something *today*, you become an obstacle for hundreds of people not yet born. Their action in the next century depends on our action today. I think that this kind of educator has to be clear about that.

It's impossible for me just to think of my dream without thinking about those who are not yet in the world. I have to have this strange feeling to love those who

190

have not come yet, in order to prepare. It is a collective practice, and it means that the presence of those who are alive today is important. Those who come tomorrow will start acting, precisely taking what we did as the starting point. This is how history can be made. Marx said men make history and are made by history, and men make history starting from some reality in which they find themselves, from the reality that they were given. We are now dealing with the present in order to create the future. We are now creating the future by the formation of the present. We are creating the *future present* for the new generation, from which they will make history. For these reasons, I think it is absolutely indispensable that educators be secure, capable, and have a capacity for loving and for curiosity.

MYLES: Curiosity is very important I think, and I think too much of education, starting with childhood education, is either designed to kill curiosity or it works out that way anyway. As you were talking, I was thinking when Charis and Thorsten were little, we had a boat on the lake, and of course to the little kids to ride in that boat was just about the epitome of anything you could find. Then there was a big bluff at the edge of the mountain, where you could break your neck if you fell off, but it was a popular place for people to go. Those were the two things they most wanted to do. Now there's a problem. How do you keep your kids from drowning in a boat or from falling off the bluff? There are two ways to deal with that problem. One is to get rid of the boat and build a fence around the bluff. That'd take care of those two. We didn't always agree on everything, as any husband and wife shouldn't, but Zilphia and I chose not to solve the problem by removing the problem, but to place restrictions on Thorsten and Charis that would make them remove the boat and build the fence within themselves. We were criticized for saying to them: "There are limits. You cannot do this." Some of our liberal educational friends said we shouldn't say no. We said: "Well, we love our kids. We're going to discipline them to learn within themselves not to do that." That was a deliberate choice.

Now I contend that the people who remove the boat take away the incentive for kids learning to swim so they can ride in the boat. They cripple them in having control and making decisions. The people who remove the boat and build the fences forget to tear them down when the kids get big enough to use them. In adult life it's the same thing. You know there are people who are never allowed to do things that they *could* do. Help people *develop* within themselves. I've carried over that way of thinking in a lot of situations. I think when educators go into an organization or a community as outside experts with the answers, they're taking the boat away or they're building the fence. They're not letting the people have to face up to dealing with their own problems, and they cripple them by not allowing them to make their own decisions.

You see, I'm getting back to what he asked. Do you tell people what you know is good for them, or do you let them flounder around and find out for themselves, maybe helping them explore possibilities? Do you set up situations in which they can learn but use that as a learning experience instead of a *telling* experience?

PAULO: Yes, but what I want to say, Myles, is that in the process of helping people *discover,* there is undoubtedly teaching.

MYLES: Sure it's teaching.

PAULO: It's impossible for me to help someone without teaching him or her something with which they can start to do by themselves. That is my own testimony of respect for them. It is consistent as a way of teaching. Not necessarily of teaching a certain content or . . .

MYLES: Or a fact.

PAULO: But immediately I need also to teach some content, do you see? I agree with you. My choice is like yours, but in trying to do what you did, maybe—in a different space, different culture, different history—less is then needed. I always was teaching. No matter that I am under the tree talking with some people. This is for me absolute. I have to assume that, you see. I have nothing against teaching. But I have many things against teaching in an authoritarian way.

THIRD PARTY: When most people talk about teaching, they talk about content as if it has a power of reality that is greater than the individual. Do you assume that what you teach about is true or are you always open to the possibility that you're wrong and that the person you're teaching may be right?

PAULO: Of course I am. I am constantly open, precisely because of the limits of the act of knowing. I am sure that knowing is historical, that it's impossible to *know* without the history of human beings. Now I don't want to discuss this question theologically. It means that it is in the social experience of history that we as human beings have created knowledge. It's because of that that we continue to recreate the knowledge we created, and create a new knowledge. If knowledge can be overcome, if the knowledge of yesterday necessarily does not make sense today and then I need another knowledge. It means that knowledge has *historicity*. That is, knowledge never is static. It's always in the process.

Then if I recognize my position as a cognitive subject, as a subject capable of knowing, my first position has to be a humble one vis-à-vis the very process of knowing, and vis-à-vis the process of learning in which I as teacher and the students as the students are engaged in at a certain moment in a certain class. I am humble not because I want to be agreeable. I don't accept being humble for tactical reasons.

THIRD PARTY: But authentically.

PAULO: Yes, I am humble because I am incomplete. Just because of that. This is not because I need people to love me, though I need that people love me, but I don't have to make any kind of trap for the love. Do you see? Then if I understand this process, I am open, absolutely open, every time to be taught by the students. Sometimes we are mistaken in our understanding of reality. We are even mistaken in our knowing of the knowledge. I don't know if it's good English, but sometimes we are mistaken in the process of *reknowing*. For example, a student suddenly says: "Professor, I think that you are wrong. This is not like this. The question is different." Then he or she satisfies you. I have had experiences like this, and it is necessary to accept that immediately and to assume a new way of speaking about the issue. Of course, to the extent that you belong to another generation, that you have been serious in the process of teaching—to the extent that you read, that you study, that you develop your curiosity—you have more possibility to clarify the search of the students, than the students have. Less experienced intellectually, they have less chance, but it does not mean that they don't have the possibility to help us.

Because of that, one of the virtues I think that we educators have to create—because I am sure also that we don't receive virtues as gifts; we make virtues not intellectually, but through practice—one of the virtues we have to create in ourselves as progressive educators is the virtue of humility.

THIRD PARTY: Myles, the reason that I asked the question of Paulo is that you said something that could sound very authoritarian, which was, "When I know something is good for people I should do something about it".

PAULO: It's a very good question.

MYLES: When I say I do something about it, what I do about it is to try to expose them to certain experiences, ways of thinking, that will lead them to take a look at what I believe in. I think when they take a look at it, there's a chance that they might come to the same conclusion. They've got to come to that conclusion *themselves*. And if I really believe in what I want people to believe in, I don't tell them about it. I don't as an authoritarian figure say you *must* believe it. I think I know much more about how people learn than that. I try to find ways to *expose* them to learning processes that would finally lead them to take a look at my conclusion. That's all I can do. Once they take a look at it, if they don't accept it, then I've gone as far as I can.

THIRD PARTY: What about the notion, though, that through the experience of working with them you may decide that what you believe was wrong, and that they may have a better perception of that than you did.

MYLES: Well I think you have to divide that into principles. When I say what I believe, I'm talking about principles such as love and democracy, where people control their lives.

THIRD PARTY: Your vision.

MYLES: My vision. Now the strategy for my vision, the approaches and processes, I've learned from other people. I'm always learning new ways of doing, but frankly, I haven't really changed my overall vision. My vision is so far off, in terms of the goal, that there's been nothing to shift my vision. For example, my vision was clarified politically during the Depression when we were faced with capitalism coming apart. There was a socialist alternative and a fascist alternative, an authoritarian and a democratic alternative. I chose at that time, out of that experience and out of my religious ethical beliefs, to opt on the side of a democratic solution to the problems, not an authoritarian solution. That's frozen into a principle. I believe in democracy versus authoritarianism. That hasn't changed. What *has* changed is an understanding of the capitalist system. If you're going to change a system, you have to understand it, and I understood it less well then than I understand it now. I've learned a lot about how you work with people, and I've learned a lot about what I like to call subvalues. Those basic principles that I want to share with people have been modified, extended—not limited—and have become more concrete in my imagination. I hold these principles more firmly than I did before, so that vision, so that long range goal is what I want to share.

As for the process of getting there, everybody has to work those things out on their own. I believe that there are many truths, many untruths, and there are many right ways to do things and many wrong ways to do things. Quite often I've said any kind of problem has five or six good solutions and five or six bad solutions. What I try to get people to do is choose one of the good ways instead of one of the bad ways, but not influence which one, because that depends on how people function, what people's backgrounds are. The people who grew up after I did, who have a different background, came to their conclusions through different processes, but their processes are as valued as mine. I don't question that.

CHAPTER 5

Education and Social Change

"You have to bootleg education"

THIRD PARTY: Education is political, but is politics educational? In our experience, if you're beginning as Highlander does, outside of the formal classroom, if you're beginning with the groups involved in social change, then . . .

PAULO: It's political.

THIRD PARTY: So where does education fit within political struggle?

MYLES: That's very interesting, especially with Paulo's premise. I think all of us at Highlander started out with the idea that we were going to do adult education. We've called our work adult education. We thought of ourselves as educators. We deliberately chose to do our education outside the schooling system. At that time, there was a lot of discussion about whether you should try to reform education, which is what we were concerned about, by working inside the system, because if you worked outside the system, you couldn't influence the system. The argument was that you could change the system. We concluded that reform within the system *reinforced* the system, or was co-opted by the system. Reformers didn't change the system, they made it more palatable and justified it, made it more humane, more intelligent. We didn't want to make that contribution to the schooling system. But we knew if we worked outside the system, we would not be recognized as educators, because an educator by definition was somebody inside the schooling system. Nevertheless, we decided we'd work outside the system and be completely free to do what we thought was the right thing to do in terms of the goals that we set for ourselves and the people we were working for. Whether we had any recognition or even if we had opposition, that wouldn't affect our position. We said we could go further in trying to experiment. We were going to experiment with ways to do social education, and we could carry on that experiment outside with more validity than we could inside the system, because we didn't have to conform to anything. Nobody could tell us what to do. We could make our own mistakes, invent our own process.

It wasn't surprising to us that we were not considered educators. We were condemned as agitators or propagandists, the most kindly condemnations, and mostly we were called communists or anarchists or whatever cuss words people could think up at the time. Interestingly enough, the people inside the school system almost unanimously said Highlander had nothing to do with education. They said we did organizing, we did propaganda. Even the people who financed and supported Highlander didn't claim we were doing education. They just liked what we were doing, but it wasn't education. And the truth about the matter is that very few people in the United States were calling what we did at Highlander education. Practically no educational institutions invited any of us to talk about education. We were invited to talk about organizing, civil rights, international problems—but education, no. We were not educators.

PAULO: You were activists.

MYLES: We were activists, yes. We were not neutral. We weren't "educators." The change came, and I think I've written you about this, after the Brazilian government made a contribution of Paulo Friere to the United States by kicking him out of Brazil. He came to Harvard, and he started talking about the experience of learning. He started talking about out-of-schooling education.

PAULO: Yes.

MYLES: And lo and behold, people started looking around and they said, "Oh, you know maybe there is something outside schools we could call education." And it was only then that people started saying Highlander was doing education. I can just practically date it. I *can* date it. Somebody who was writing a book about Paulo asked me several years ago what I thought his greatest contribution to the United States was, and I told them that as far as I was concerned his greatest contribution was to get people in academic circles to recognize there's such

a thing as experiential education. So I think when Highlander was first recognized to the extent that we were
invited to talk about education was after Paulo made
this kind of education respectable by being a professor
at Harvard.

THIRD PARTY: But you had done the Citizenship Schools,
and you called those "schools," and you had been involved in the international adult education movements.

MYLES: *We* always called it education. I'm just saying the
"schooling" people never called it education. We always
thought it was the best education. We didn't have any
problem about this, but we weren't recognized by *academicians* as doing education.

When we did our Citizenship Schools in the fifties,
they were recognized as being successful in teaching
people to read and write. People wrote articles about
it, talked about it, and everybody knew people were
learning to read and write. They still wouldn't call it
education because Highlander was doing it outside the
system. That's my whole point. That the word education didn't include out-of-school learning. It never
bothered us in the sense that we weren't dependent on
their acceptance—not that we didn't want their good
will and not that we didn't *have* a lot of their good will.

PAULO: But Myles I would like to come back a little bit to the
question of working inside of the system and outside
of the system. I think that if we ask ourselves what we
mean by system, we discover that when we are speaking
about the *educational* system. In fact, we are speaking
about a *subsystem* in relation with the big system, the
productive system, the political system, the structural

system. For example, as a fantastic educator you were always creating these extraordinary spaces—political, cultural, and educational spaces within the system—as you have since the 1930s with Highlander. If we consider this in relation to the system, of course we discover that it is out of the subsystem of education but that it is inside of the system.

MYLES: I'm talking about the school system. I'm talking about the schooling system, not the social system.

PAULO: Yes, but for me, Myles, there is another aspect. The ideal is to fight against the system taking the two fronts, the one internal to the schooling system and the one external to the schooling system. Of course, we have much space outside the schooling system, much more space to work, to make decisions, to choose. We have more space outside the system, but we also can create the space *inside* of the subsystem or the schooling system in order to occupy the space. That is, I think politically, every time we can occupy some position inside of the subsystem, we should do so. But as much as possible, we should try to establish good relationships with the experience of people outside the system in order to help what we are trying to do inside. The intimacy of the schooling system is so bureaucratized that sometimes we despair; that is, after two, three, four, ten years of working, we don't see complete results of our efforts and we begin not to believe anymore. Even though I recognize that out of the schooling system there is more space, I think that it is necessary to invent ways to work together or to work inside of the system. It's not easy.

MYLES: B-F, "Before Freire," not only did we not get in

the universities, but they sometimes kicked anybody out who supported Highlander. So that's a big political change. It's your educational ideas helping in this country to create space for this kind of work.

At the beginning, back when Highlander started, there was a lot of radical ferment. The country was in a period of flux, and it was a very creative period in this country, the most creative period I think that I've lived through. There were half a dozen experimental colleges started at that time. There were Bard, Sarah Lawrence, later Black Mountain, a little later on Goddard. Highlander was started about the same time. And since we were all experimental and new and had no recognition, we used to have good relationships. Three or four of those schools would send their staff members to Highlander for an orientation or would send their students every year. We had good relationships for the first several years there, until they got a little bit stuffy and a little cautious and got more into academics. There were professors who were supportive of Highlander in the thirties, and they kept on supporting Highlander. But they couldn't get the institution to even allow me to speak there, and they were heads of departments. I'm not going to say we didn't have friends. I'm just saying institutions, except those early institutions, didn't have any place for Highlander.

Now I also should say that all along there have been individuals in universities all over the United States and Canada with whom we worked comfortably. But I'm talking about the fact that I could be invited publicly and they'd announce it. That didn't happen. They used

Education and Social Change

to invite me, and then didn't want anyone to know it till I got away, and then they denied it after I was there.

In the meantime, we were working with individuals and helping them kind of subvert the system. We were always doing that. We were always accused—and justly, you know—of trying to subvert by working with people.

Here in the mountains we have had moonshiners and bootleggers, people who make illegal whiskey and sell it. They don't pay taxes, and they're called bootleggers. They used to put a pint of whiskey in their boots back in the old days and when they'd walk up to somebody who'd buy it, they'd reach down in their boot and take it out and sell it to them. So the phrase I've always used when I talk is, "You have to bootleg education." You have to find a way to bootleg it. It's illegal, really, because it's not proper, but you do it anyway. We worked with a lot of people who bootlegged education. That's always been going on. I don't want to give the impression that we have been isolated or that we haven't had financial support. We weren't recognized as "education."

THIRD PARTY: Well both of you, in both places, were exiled, right? The difference is that in Latin America they exile physically by pushing guns. Here in the United States exile takes another form, freezing ideas out or closing you down. The old Highlander, as you know, was not here in this location. It was seized and destroyed by the state in 1959 because of the educational work during the McCarthy period. So I am struck actually that what you've been saying is that the system, overall system, found a way to exile both forms of education, and now there seems to be some new space opening up within both situations. And some recognition; you've both received awards. We worry sometimes, are we becoming too legitimate? Does that mean our ideas, our work is being co-opted, that it's no longer on the cutting edge? Does success mean that we're no longer subversive enough?

PAULO: No, no. First of all concerning this question, which is very important, of co-optation: of course it is impossible for power to exist without trying to co-opt the other side, which is not yet powered. Do you see? It takes part of the struggle. Trying to co-opt is a kind of a struggle on behalf of those who have power to do so. It's a tactic; it's a moment of the struggle. It's very interesting because there are people who continue to say that there should be no struggle; above all, we should get along together. If we speak about class struggle, then many people begin to be afraid, but reality is just like this. Co-optation is a tactical moment of the struggle.

Secondly, in order for you not to be co-opted, at least for you to be out of the possibility of some power wanting to co-opt you, it's necessary that you do nothing. The choice is between doing nothing in order not to be co-opted, or doing something in order to be an object of co-optation. I prefer to be an object of co-optation. Right now what I have to do is to fight to understand co-optation as a moment of the struggle, and to give my attention to the attempt by others to co-opt my ideas.

Another thing. Thinking about the history of a society: not because I am in his house, but I consider Myles's contribution to history as much much bigger. (I don't say that I also did not give. I know that I have made some contribution so it's not false modesty.) Myles became himself by struggling and not the opposite. In some moment of his struggle, some, maybe most, of his ideas were considered as something absolutely impossible to be even thought and then never accepted. He started, for example, discussing putting into practice the struggle against racism when it was a kind of cataclysm, an earthquake. Illegal. In this place here, Highlander, which is also history, he committed disobedience, no?

I did something in Brazil in the fifties and sixties that also was considered an absurdity: to say that the illiterate peasants should have the right to vote. Brazil had been always governed by intellectuals. But what happens is that historically the change has come, and some of the change has come precisely because of a struggle like Myles gives here. What he said thirty to forty years ago could provoke jail, repression, and discrimination. Today, even though they are not yet accepted totally, his ideas begin to become obvious. Then this means that, politically speaking, and historically speaking, the space begins to become greater. Then we have more meters and sometimes some kilometers to walk on. This is the question, because if it was not possible to change the *comprehension* of the facts, it would be impossible to work, and then it is not because we changed. It is not because we are no longer fighting. This is *because* our fight, the fight of many, many, many others, provoked a legal change.

Also the fight of other peoples was seen, for example, to work in Brazil, in Latin America, in general before Cuba. The other thing was to work after Cuba. One thing was to fight before Nicaragua. The other thing is to fight today. I know I understand for example, what it means for these fantastic people from Nicaragua to have done what they did and to continue to do what they are doing. Nicaragua, to the extent that the people of Nicaragua got their history into their hands, have begun to reinvent their society. The people in Nicaragua are helping us in Brazil, are helping us as Latin Americans, and are helping you to the extent that you are also helping them. This is kind of a struggle here; on the one hand, you gave support to Nicaragua. On the other hand, you made an impression in the space inside of the country, do you see, and this is history. The change is inside and outside. You ask whether we changed a lot, whether or not we have been co-opted. What happened for me is history also. It does not mean that we have the right to stop. The people who continued to struggle while I was in exile made it possible for me to go back to Brazil. Not because I was out of Brazil; it was not my exile that sent me again back to Brazil. It was the role of those who stayed in Brazil, the fighting that brought me and the others into Brazil again, but into a different Brazil, historically speaking—in spite of the bad circumstances we still have in Brazil today.

MYLES: What opportunities do you have with this acceptance now to influence the parts of Brazil other than where you are? I mean what kind of outreach is possible now?

PAULO: I don't want to emphasize the importance of my work. I have recognized the work of many other Brazilian educators who differ from me. But I can tell you that more and more, in different parts of Brazil, the people are working and recreating me and reinventing me, adapting to the new circumstances of the country and putting into practice some of the ideas I have defended until today. Recently, for example, I spent four days in Recife. I was working three days with a team of educators. Television and newspaper reporters asked me, in interview, about how I was experiencing that moment, because I was expelled from the state and now the government is the same government that was expelled in 1964. The governor was reelected. Of course I said it is a reason for me to be happy, to feel well, not to feel proud, but happy. I see many many places in Brazil today, in the north of the country, the south of the country, where there are many many kinds of work with my ideas. I am allowed in the country. It is good.

MYLES: Now how much of a turnover has there been from the early days, through the base community groups? I know that when I was down about ten years ago in Rio and São Paulo and Recife, there was a lot of activity, especially among a lot of priests and bishops. I met Dom Cammera [the Cardinal of São Paulo] and Cardinal Arness [the retired Archbishop of Olinda and Recife]. Through them I met some of the priests who were out in the rural areas, where officials tried to close their churches. I remember I went to one Catholic church not so far from a little town right outside of Rio. The church was full of flowers almost up to the altar, so I asked the priest where the people sat to come to be blessed, and he said: "Oh, they don't come here anymore. This church is for weddings and things like that; we don't use it for worship." I said, "Is this your church?" He said, "No, my church is out in these communities, that's where the church is now." He was using his church for a storehouse. Now most people—people like that who are out working these base community groups or working with the unions at a time when it was illegal for the unions to have meetings and to have strikes—they were obviously either influenced directly or indirectly by some of the things you'd done there and in Chile. I don't know how much there was of that, but there was some, and I've been told there's been quite a carryover of the ideas, of course adapted, reinterpreted, as they should be, but still some of the ideas there. Did you have any sense when you went back that this had taken place and was still a factor in their thinking?

PAULO: Yes.

MYLES: When you left, you left something behind—that's what I'm trying to say.

PAULO: Yes, yes, of course, and when I went back to Brazil, I could perceive some very interesting and strong historical changes in Brazil, some novel changes—for example, the Christian base communities. Historically from the *Christian* point of view, it is very old, but historically from the *political* point of view, it was very novel in Brazil. One of the new things I found is that the Christian people come to the churches in order to know better about their situation in relation to their faith. It

210

was very interesting to see how the people, the Christian peasants and workers, did not forget. Where sometimes they stop and only listen to the priests reading the Gospels, they began to read the Gospels themselves and then began something like the circles you have in Scandinavia.

MYLES: Study circles.

PAULO: Study circles. They began also to have their study circles, studying, discussing the Gospels, and thinking about the political and social circumstances in which they were reinterpreting the Gospels. In doing that, they discovered the need to change the country, and they got a new consciousness—a historical, political consciousness of the reality. At the same time they taught the priests how to rethink the whole thing of politics and social movements and so on. Inside of this movement, some priests and some educators had read my writings. For example, I know that when it was not possible in Brazil to publish *Pedagogy of the Oppressed*, many people read the Italian edition, the French edition, the Spanish edition. Those editions multiplied in copies, and it started the book underground. Generally one of the great problems exiled people have is that they don't want to die, politically speaking. I never died because I was not exclusively a politician. I was mainly an educator who was a politician. I never died; I always was alive in Brazil, because of the books and articles and so on. It would be a mistake and show a lack of humility if I said that I was instrumental in the development of the base communities. No, I was not. But I also cannot

211

say that I did *not* have any kind of influence. No, I had a good influence, but within the limits in which I could be influential. Yes.

MYLES: I was interested in the unions when I visited Brazil earlier. Of course the unions couldn't meet unless it was an official meeting, which meant that the unions were organized in a kind of a syndicalism. All the steel workers in the whole area were in one local union, ten to twelve thousand, and they only had four or five shop stewards. There might be twenty plants, so most of the plants didn't even have any representation. But there was a kind of unofficial movment outside the official unions. There were the people the priests were working with, and in fact a lot of their plans, their protests and even strikes were planned in these base communities. They'd pray a while and read a little scripture and then get down to business.

PAULO: Look, I think that the political consciousness of the working class in Brazil today has gained clarity; it is very interesting how many dimensions of the working class are perceiving the political and the social process. I don't want to say that we already have very good participation from the point of view of mobilization, of organization, but maybe I can say without risking a mistake that, above all, in urban centers like São Paulo, we have a great part of the working class in the unions, for example, movements grasping fundamental aspects of history. For example, I think that in the process of struggle we spoke about before—not necessarily with guns, but the struggle because of differences in the antagonist's interests—there is a qualitative difference when the leaders of the working class discover something that is very obvious, that is, that the education that the dominant classes offer to the working class necessarily is the education that reproduces the working class as such. Look, I don't want to say that *every time* the education that the ruling class offers to the working class reproduces the working class as such. Maybe sometimes education does not get this result, but the *ideological* intention of the ruling class could not be another one. If it was another one, we could no longer understand the contradictions in social life. But for me, this moment of new understanding is a very important moment in the struggle of the working class.

Right now, it's very good for me to tell you that in about 1986 I was elected president of the council of the Institute of Cajamar. Cajamar is the name of the region. Some groups of workers there got a building that used to be a great motel on the road to Campinas. In this wonderful building they created an institute for formation or training of the working class, peasants and the urban workers under their responsibility. They had the help of some intellectuals whose political choice coincides with their choice, also intellectuals who don't think that they possess the truths to give to the workers. Intellectuals who respect the workers' process of knowing and who want to grow up with the workers. I am the president of this institution today. Next year I hope to be able to give much more presence to the work and to make a bigger contribution. They are offering weekend seminars to the working class. People who come to the institute can live inside of the house. It's a big building,

213

120 or so rooms, and there is a kitchen, and they have entertainment. There are teachers who come from the working class and there are teachers from the university, and they organize programs about the history of the country, the history of the working class in Brazil, of the struggle of the working class, how to understand critically history in Brazil.

So this institute is making a very important contribution to the working class movement and to the struggle of the people. It is a kind of a seed for a popular university. That is, it is not a question of transforming this institute into a university less efficient than universities we already have. No, it is not the question to copy the model of the university, the formalism of the university, but this is precisely what I said in the beginning of our conversation. It is a center that wants to be a theoretical context *inside* of which the workers can make a critical reflection about what they do *outside* of the theoretical context. That is what they are doing in the concrete context or even inside of the union context. That is, they get distance, inside of the theoretical context, from the struggle outside in order to understand it better, to understand the reason for the struggle and to make better methods for this struggle, and how to choose. It is this need of transforming society and how to do that. It means to be patient, or the words I prefer, to be impatiently patient, in the process of struggling to change.

"The people begin to get their history into their hands, and then the role of education changes"

PAULO: Today, I think, Myles, there is another perception that comes up in the process of struggle, which is the perception of the right that the workers have to express their suffering. I don't know. Maybe some reader of this book that we are speaking today will say: "But Paulo, it does not make sense. It is nothing, the right of expressing pain." Yes, I think that it is a *fantastic* right. Do you see? Not just individually but socially. We have the right to say that we are suffering; we have the right to express our pain. When Elza died, I had the right to stay at home, suffering. The university understood that I could not go there to give a seminar. But I asked myself during those so difficult days for me, how many workers could cry about *their* loss? How many workers could *choose* to do as I when I dealt with my loss, with the loss of Elza, with my sorrow? Then it is a fundamental right. Of course, first of all we have to get the right of eating. Of course, we have to get the right of sleeping, of living in a house, and we are very far away from that still in Brazil. But we have to get more and more space for rights like this. We have to have the right of commanding our education, the education we need, and also we have to get the right to express our suffering because, look, the workers suffer. You can define the life of the workers, of the popular people, as a struggle. They struggle to survive. And in some moment, then, you get the need to express this right, to live this right. We are not yet at this level, but at least the workers are

215

beginning to struggle, to fight in order to get their education or part of it into their hands. This is for me a very new moment in Brazilian political history. It has to do also with the creation in Brazil of a workers party with leadership of workers, with the presence of many intellectuals. I hope that many of us are learning how difficult it is to make history, and how important it is to learn that we are being made *by* the history we make in the social process inside of history. Fortunately I am not naively optimistic, idealistic, but I *am* critically optimistic, with the process of learning that a great part of the working class demonstrates today in Brazil.

We are in the sight of a process. I always say that the deepened transformation in society never arrived on a second Monday morning. Never. No, the radical transformation of society is a *process*, really, and it comes like this.

MYLES: I've often said that if we could do something overnight, it's not worth doing because if it's that simple and that easy, it'll take care of itself. There'll be plenty of people who will see that it happens. Tough problems take time and you have to struggle with them.

THIRD PARTY: Is this struggle to put education in the hands of the people? Is that what's perhaps most significant about Nicaragua in your context, Paulo? Myles has also visited Nicaragua.

PAULO: Yes. I would say something about that, and afterwards I would like very much to hear Myles speaking about Nicaragua and what he can do as challenger of other people. It's very, very interesting. It has to do with something that I said before. The revolution in Nicaragua did not happen like this, in an instance. That is, the leader was killed in 1934, and the revolution got power in 1979, and it continues. But what is interesting to see is how things changed in the country. How the nature of the process began to change, to get a new face, a new quality. Of course, precisely because the event is a historical phenomenon, it cannot be explained mechanistically. If we could change a society like we can change the position of the furniture of this house, it would be fantastic. It would be just a question of muscular power, no? That is, I can take this chair and put it over there. We could change everything here in ten minutes. History is not like this. It takes time in history to make history. You cannot make it today, but the change comes up in all directions and dimensions of the life of society. Nevertheless it is easier in some corners of society's historical streets. It's less easy in other corners. The corner of education is not so easy to change because there is strong and heavy ideological material that has been transmitted, even to the revolutionaries. For example, there is a certain authoritarian traditionalism or traditional totalitarianism that was very alive many years before, centuries before the revolution, which had false conviviality inside of the very revolutionaries. There is sometimes a certain contradiction between the speech of a revolutionary and his or her practice. As an educator, for example, he or she is much more traditional and fears the students' possibilities more than he or she should. They could believe much more in the abilities of the students, of the people, but they are afraid of freedom. They are conditioned by a very old fear,

217

which is the fear of freedom. It happens, and you cannot change by *decree* one of the obstacles for the creation of the new education, which is precisely the presence, the *alive* presence, of all this kind of ideology.

It is a time of confrontation, this transition, the time of transition of the old society to a new one that does not exist yet, but it's being created with the confrontation of the ghosts. There are many ghosts in society fighting against the dream of a much more open society. Generally revolutions have this in common. We cannot decide this period cannot exist. We have to understand that it exists historically, culturally, socially. We must fight also. The struggle does not stop when the revolution is in power. It starts a new kind of struggle, new kind of fighting that all societies knew and are knowing. Then the role of education changes also in this new period.

But what I want to say is that with the greater difficulties in education's corner of history, society nevertheless begins to change qualitatively and the people begin to experience that the time now is different from the other time. Then the people begin to know that there is a new space created by the social work, social transformations that society is experiencing, is living. It means what I said before. The people begin to get their history into their hands, and then the role of education changes. Before they got in power, education was the *official* education; the schooling system was an attempt to reproduce the dominant ideology of the ruling class. The revolutionary groups, the progressive groups, worked in education in order to demystify the official role of education. Now the question is not for the new education to become a kind of indoctrination, it is as political as the other one was political, but now with another direction with another dream. That is, the emphasis now, in the process of transition of revolution, is to create an education that enlarges and amplifies the horizon of critical understanding of the people, to create an education devoted to freedom. I am sure that this is the opinion and the position and the struggle of Fernando Cardenal as minister of education in Nicaragua. I am sure that Fernando has to be patient also with some resistance from the right and from the left. I am not saying that he must be in the center—no, he must be a left man, but with this kind of ideological resistance. I think that this is one of the imperatives with which Nicaragua lives now, demanding a very open and creative education, working to increase certainty about the role of the people in the process of creating, of transforming power and of knowing their society, their reality, in order to participate as never the people have participated before.

MYLES: How much has the schooling system—not popular education, but the schools themselves—changed?

PAULO: It is not easy to change. I am sure that if you ask this question to Fernando he will tell you seriously things like I heard from President Nyerere, for example, in the seventies in Tanzania. When I talked with the president, he used to say to me, "Paulo, it's not easy to put into practice the things we think about." Yes, it is not easy, but it's not impossible. This is my conviction.

The question for Nicaragua as well as for Cuba is how to deal with this resistance the day after the revolution got power. If it was mechanistic, it should be very easy, but it is not. For example, one of the fears we have here as educators is the fear of experiencing new things, of exposing ourselves to mistakes. In the last analysis we have real freedom. We are afraid of risking. And it's impossible, just impossible, to create without risking. It's absolutely impossible, but it takes time to begin to risk. We must be free; we must be free to believe in freedom. Do you see this paradox? Without freedom it's difficult to understand freedom. On the other hand, we fight for freedom to the extent that we don't have freedom, but in fighting for freedom we discover how freedom is beautiful and difficult to be created, but we have to believe that it's *possible*.

I don't accept that the school in itself is bad. We need to go beyond a metaphysical understanding of the school. For me the school is a social and historical institution, and in being a social and historical institution, the school can be changed. But the school can be changed not exclusively by a decree, but by a new generation of teachers, of educators who must be prepared, trained, formed.

I don't like the word *training* in English. Maybe it's a prejudice of mine, but I prefer *formation, formation* in French and *formação* in Portuguese. One of the most important tasks I think for a revolutionary government or a progressive government—because I don't want to leave out of this reflection the people who did not have a revolution, like my people—for educators and politicians, is to think seriously about the formation of the educators. But understanding formation not as something that we do in some weekends or some semesters, but formation as a permanent process, and formation as being an exercise, a critical understanding of what we do. That is, getting the practice we have, the experience we have, and then reflecting on the experience and the practice in order to understand theoretically what it means. We should form groups or teams of supervisors to follow very near as friends and as people who must know more than the teachers in order to challenge the teachers about what they are doing. Then, through this kind of very strong serious work, through a work that is at the same time tender and heavy and serious and rigorous, we need to shape, to reshape, to form permanently the teachers without manipulating them.

MYLES: But it's quite obvious that a revolution to my knowledge has not changed any schooling system or any that I've ever known about. School systems stay pretty much like they were before.

PAULO: Yes.

MYLES: It happened in Cuba, happened in Nicaragua.

PAULO: But, Myles, I was in Cuba in June, and I spent four hours one morning with the national team that is in charge of transforming the schooling system, and I liked very much the issues we discussed. I also met a physicist, a very good scientist, who told me that the minister of education invited some scientists to discuss education in Cuba. And the minister asked the scientists two questions. The first, what seemed to the scientists to be wrong in the educational system? And, second, what would they suggest? They said the worst thing in the system is some traditional totalitarianism—this is the thing we were talking about—and the best thing to do should be, through teaching the contents, to challenge the students to think critically. Do you see? Could you have another better answer? No. It is just that, but it is also history. Maybe if those questions had been asked ten years ago, another scientist would not have answered like this.

MYLES: I don't mean to say that they aren't changing. I meant that the revolution didn't automatically change the schooling system in any country that I know of. It opened up the possibility of change, but it didn't just change it like it changed some other things. It changed the land ownership, changed voting, changed a lot of things as a direct result of the revolution. Schools don't change automatically in any place I know of.

PAULO: It's another example of how the transformation of society, in being historical, is not mechanistic. It's not a question just of wanting to do differently. Of course, it implies a political decision, but it implies also a very clear ability to use *time* to make change. Do you see? Things can be taught inside of history, not before time, but in time, on time. There is time for all these things.

MYLES: Since the revolution doesn't change the schooling system, how do you go about changing? What has been done to change it? That process is very important because if schools can't change when you have a revolution or don't change, then it's going to slow down the fruition of the revolution. It's terribly important, and it's

no answer to say in Nicaragua we've got a popular education movement, because the parents still send their
kids to the same schools. It's still the place that's part of
the old structure.

I know that if we're going to move in the direction
of radical social change, we've got to take a further step
than we're talking about here. I could illustrate what
I'm talking about by an experience I had when I was
invited to be one of the official election observers in
Nicaragua. They invited people from all over the world
to be there to observe the election. They wanted people
to see for themselves. We had a little badge that meant
we could go in any polling place in Nicaragua before
they opened the office to see that there's no stuffed bal-
lot boxes. We could help count the ballots. We could
be there when people were voting. I did some of all
those things. But I wanted to do more than just observe
the election, because I knew the election was going to
be an honest election, and I was glad to be a witness
to the fact. I asked to be allowed to join the Witnesses
for Peace up on the border between Sandino and the
Honduran border. I spent that day within sight of Honduras in little farm communities, little school houses
where the voting was going on. In fact, we were in such
an isolated part of the country that they hadn't gotten
around to delivering the ballots. We took the ballots
into the places so they could vote. We went in a four-
wheel Jeep, and then we walked. The whole business
had been wiped out by the contras, but in that area
popular education was going on, under the gun, right

there within sight. I kept looking up in the mountains, because if you were on top of those mountains, that was in Honduras.

In that situation I met three or four popular educators. Two days before, they had found this popular educator who lived nearby with his throat cut, which was what the contras did to popular educators to let people know that they knew they were popular educators. (Not so incidentally the CIA claimed to be the policymaker for the contras.) As I looked at that man's grave, that simple grave where his neighbors had buried him with a little wooden cross on top, I was filled with tears and filled with anger, knowing that our government was really responsible for that man's death. But the fact that there were people even within sight of that house who were continuing to do popular education meant that they had moved way beyond what we've talked about up to now, in terms of being effective and reaching the people. They had committed their lives to it.

And you know I'm raising the question, can we move in this country? Can the people in Appalachia who are so impressed with popular education and what's going on in Nicaragua, can we move another stage beyond just thinking it's a wonderful idea and be willing to make sacrifices? Now I'm not saying that that's something that's going to happen tomorrow or should happen tomorrow, because there's no basis for it, but if we moved in that direction, if we would move to the place where we are willing to enter acts of civil disobedience . . . Many people in this region have already signed a pledge saying that they would be able to take part in acts of civil disobedience and go to jail for this. So we're moving in the direction, but I think we have to really add another dimension to what we've been talking about, and that's the courage of these people who are continuing to do this popular education there despite what we are doing to them. That's a dimension that I don't think we've gotten into here in Appalachia or at Highlander, but one we must get into if we're going to move toward any kind of transformation of society. That's another lesson I'd like us to learn from the Nicaraguan popular educators.

I don't have any fear that it won't take place. I've seen it in the civil rights movement. The people I was involved with in the civil rights movement who were willing to die for what they believed in I had known five years before, and they were frivolous, actually frivolous. A movement can change people. So I'm not hopeless. I'm just saying I think we have to realize that we have to be prepared to help people move to that stage when the time comes, and I think people will move. I don't think there's any question. They've done it in the struggles in the coal fields and the union. There's no question about people being willing to do it. That's a side of popular education that we very seldom hear people talk about, but I wanted to be sure that we understood that that's the price some of those people have to pay and are paying.

PAULO: It is a very serious point and I think that we would have the risk here in this conversation to be considered as maybe two old men full of illusions and hopes, when we say things like this. But it is important to call to the attention of the young people that being a progressive on one hand does not mean to be naive, but to make some decisions and then to risk the preservation of the revolution. On the other hand, being a progressive means to deepen the connection with the masses of people, means to respect the beliefs of the people, means to consult the people, means to start from the letters and words with which the people are starting the process of education. All these things are like recognizing what levels of knowledge people have, in order to create a new knowledge and to help the people to know better what they already know. It's not an idealism; it is consistency. It's a revolutionary process.

MYLES: This is heavy listening.

CHAPTER 6

Reflections

"Peaks and valleys and hills and hollers"

PAULO: And now, Myles, I would like to ask you a very personal question. What were the first reasons that brought you into the roads of this kind of struggle, believing in human beings of all races? You are a beautiful white man with blue eyes and tall, and you had every reason not to do what you did, from the point of view of the world. What were some of the reasons? Maybe a strong desire of love? Maybe some religious beliefs? Maybe some political clarities, philosophical ideas? Say something about this.

MYLES: Well, I really don't know the answer.

PAULO: Sometimes I ask myself, and I also don't know.

MYLES: I could think of some periods that stand out in re-energizing me or sending me off at a different angle.

I don't think any two or three of them would explain completely.

Somehow I think it was a combination of my parents' interest in education and their nonoppressive religious beliefs. They weren't "churchy" kind of people, although they went to church—I think as much for social reasons as any other reasons, because there wasn't anything else to do in a little town except go to church and go to school, or for the men to sit around the barber shop and talk. But there were values involved, educational values, ethical values, religious values, social values—not explicit, but there. And I think poverty and having to work can have a good effect or a bad effect. To some people it dries them up and makes them feel that there's no hope. (Hopeless people make good fascists.) But for some reason I was educated positively by that experience. Before I was in high school, I was aware that while we didn't feel poor in spirit, we were deprived. We didn't have money to buy books, and my brother and I—Delmas, my brother who's dead now—both liked to read. We found out that you could order books five books for a dollar from Sears and Roebuck catalog, and if they didn't have the books you ordered, they'd send you other books. If you didn't like the books they sent you, send them back and they would send you some more books. So we never liked any book they sent us! We used one dollar for two years. Just kept sending them back. We didn't care what they sent us, and we figured out that they were such a big outfit that they'd never check. They finally found out and said there weren't any more for our dollar. But they gave us the books.

But no, we were deprived except where we could find some way to gnaw off the arm of the system a little bit. That deprivation was not so much a deprivation of spirit as much as not having a proper diet, not being able to buy books or have the clothes to go to social affairs. So we had to live within ourselves, which was not a bad thing. My sympathies have always been directed outward. I can remember very well during college, when I was working in the mountains, in the Cumberland Mountains about eighty miles from here, there was a train that ran through the mountains, through gorges and mountain sides and down streams. A beautiful trip. Every time I had a chance, I would like to take that trip in the train. I would stand in between the cars and open the door so I could see out, get the breeze, and watch the mountains go by. I used to play a game. I was a giant running on the mountains, and I had to look where I put my foot because I'd come up with this peak, and I'd have to stand on the side of the next mountain. It was kind of a game of running along with the train over the mountains. I was playing that game one time, and suddenly I realized that there was a house right there. I lost interest in my little game and started looking at that house right near the tracks. As we got closer I saw a 15-year-old girl standing on the porch, hanging by one arm around the pillar that held up the porch, hanging there looking at that train with the most forlorn look I think I have ever seen.

Such a sad look. I just said to myself, she sees this train going by, and to her it represents getting away from that poverty that's drying her up. No hope. Nothing. No future. This train could take her away but she doesn't have the money to get on this train, or she wouldn't know where to go if she got on it. I started crying right there because it was such a sad picture of hopelessness. That picture stayed in my mind and is still in mind, and I still cry when I think about it. That helped me understand the cruelty of the system that blighted what could've been a beautiful life. That helped, in a way, my determination to try to do something about that situation.

But when I told that story to a friend of mine, he said: "Well now, you helped one young woman and another young man you found in the mountains go to school. Why don't you go back and find that girl and get her in school." I said: "No. She represents something else to me. She represents all the people in the mountains and to get her into school wouldn't solve the problem that she raises in my mind. It isn't an individual solution. There's no individual solution to her problem. There's many other people I could've seen, just like her. Until I can start thinking in terms of how you deal with more than one person at a time on an individual basis, then I'm not responding to the feeling I had." You know, that kind of experience was important.

Another experience that was very important to me, that moved me along in my thinking, happened at Cum-

berland College, where I was a student, in Lebanon,
Tennessee. The head of the local woolen mill was a
very reactionary manufacturer, so reactionary that he
started a southern manufacturer's organization because
he felt the national manufacturer's association was com-
munistic. This is a matter of record. I invited him later
on to come to Highlander and meet with a labor organizer and have a debate about unions, and he wrote to
his constituents in his organization that the Highlander
Folk School is the greatest insult ever known to Anglo-
Saxon purity. But it was this man, the president of the
woolen mill and a board member of Cumberland College, who was invited to give a Labor Day speech at the
university, that was in about 1926 or 1927. He said these
northern agitators are coming down here trying to stir
up the people and start unions, and we've got to keep
them out of here. He says they're going to destroy the
South. They're going to destroy industry, destroy jobs
for people. And he says God has given us the responsibility as owners of factories to provide jobs for people,
and it's up to us to decide what those jobs are, how long
people work, and what they get paid. Well, having come
from a working-class background, I almost wanted to
pull him off the platform and beat him up! It was such
an insulting thing to say.

That had a very good influence on me; it really af-
fected me in terms of my thinking about the economic
system. I could go on and on thinking of experiences
that continued to move me in a certain direction. I had
this sense that it wasn't mean individuals who caused

poverty or injustice; I just didn't have it in any kind of context. I didn't know any sociology. I knew nothing about Marx. I had no way of analyzing. Even after I was out of college, the year after I graduated, I stayed and worked in the mountains. I was still struggling with this problem of social as against individual problems and individual versus social morality, how values could be made part of the system and how they were always rejected by the system like they were a bad disease. When I discovered the Marxist way of analyzing, a sociological way of looking at things, that gave me some categories for thinking. Before, I didn't have any kind of framework. I had the right sensitivity but I didn't have any way of naming anything. That's when I found that it was absolutely necessary to understand the nature of society. If I was going to change it, going to try to do anything about it, I had to understand it. That was the beginning of a whole new insight.

Prior to that time, I had an idea that I would get a job teaching in a mountain college site. I was offered several jobs by colleges even before I graduated, because I had been working in the mountains. I was just assuming that there were ways I could work within the system. I found out that all these schools, without exception, never took the student into consideration. They always had a canned program they'd open up and dump on people. This could be religious or it could be vocational, but it was fitting the people into the colleges' conception instead of education related to the people themselves. None of them dealt with economic and social issues.

They could have been in Long Island or they could have been in Timbuktu. That's when I said I'm not going to try to fit into this situation; I'm going to try to figure out some better way of doing it.

All these contradictions that I saw had to be resolved. I think more important than how I went about resolving them is the feeling that had become a part of me, the feeling that I had to do something about injustice and it had to be done *not* on an individual basis. This feeling became so much a part of me that I never even thought about it anymore. Because of that little experience in the clover patch when I was growing up, I wasn't so much personally involved in thinking of myself. I was beginning to get my personal satisfactions out of dealing some way with this economic-political situation. To me that was where I got my joy, where I got my excitement, where I felt recompensed. So I wasn't starving myself at all. I was feeding myself all that time. My personal interests were well served; Myles Horton was never neglected in this process. Never, never. I was always terribly excited and invigorated by learning things. Sometimes I'd learn something and I couldn't sleep at night, I was so excited about what I'd learned. That to me was plenty of joy, plenty of feeling of accomplishment. People asked me why didn't I ever attempt to make it in the system, to get recognition, and my answer has always been that I did but it's in my system, not the system they're talking about. I've got my own system I had to get credit for. I always said I'd never compete with anybody but Myles Horton. All the needs that were ever very important to me, I could satisfy within my way of living and doing things, so I've never felt that I made any sacrifices.

Now it would be a great sacrifice for me if I had to yield to the system. That would be a sacrifice, not doing what I'm doing. I've had too much pleasure, too much fun doing what I have done to be given credit for it. You know, Paulo says all these complimentary things about me, and I'm glad he feels that way because I'm glad he values what I do, but I know that as insightful and as caring as Paulo is, that it isn't Paulo, but history that's going to make a decision as to whether I've done anything worthwhile.

PAULO: I think that I understand that. In the last analysis, you are a man who experiences simultaneously peace because of what you have done and the opposite of being in peace. Anxious, no? See, you experienced simultaneously peace and then anxiety.

MYLES: Don't you?

PAULO: Yes.

MYLES: Of course you do.

PAULO: Because on one hand you are more or less sure that you did the best.

MYLES: I'm on the right track. I'm sure I'm on the right track. I haven't gotten too far but I'm on the right track.

PAULO: On the other hand, you know that it's possible to do more. You cannot accept being immobilized because you think that you've finished. You experience the very nature of being a human being—that is, unfinished, constantly in search.

MYLES: When you're finished you're dead.

PAULO: Yes. And perhaps you do not finish. Nevertheless you remain in the thoughts of those who discuss you and your work. Today you talked a lot about the past, about people who are no longer here, but *you* are here.

MYLES: Let me just say one more thing. I don't have any hesitancy in using everything I can learn from you, and I have the responsibility to learn everything I can from you. Now I try to give recognition not because I think that I am obligated to, but because I want people to identify the source of this information for their own sake, so they can profit by that storehouse of knowledge. But I feel that all knowledge should be in the free-trade zone. Your knowledge, my knowledge, everybody's knowledge should be made use of. I think people who refuse to use other people's knowledge are making a big mistake. Those who refuse to share their knowledge with other people are making a great mistake, because we need it all. I don't have any problem about ideas I got from other people. If I find them useful, I'll just ease them right in and make them my own.

PAULO: Myles, I think it is so beautiful, your life and the life of this institution, because we see the cycles of work. In the thirties, the commitment was to the problems of unions, which was also education and politics. Afterward we see as a continuation of that a new source, which is the question of literacy, the question of literacy associated to the restrictions of racism. This brought you and the institution years later to the civil rights struggle. All these different moments indicate that you have been always going around the problem of dignity of human beings—the question of freedom, the dreams of the people, the respect for the people, in which education for you is shaped. For you there is no education out of that. You recognize that there are many other people who tried precisely using education to work against dignity, but it's not for you or for us.

Now I think that it would be interesting to listen to you talk a little bit about the cycles, which constitute the road of Highlander Center, telling us some thing about the thirties, the fifties, and today.

MYLES: Well, this is one way I have talked about it: High-lander's always been in the mountainous part of the United States, and our history at Highlander has been an up and down history, peaks and valleys and hills and hollers. The history of Highlander is the same as the history of the South. Our history is a reflection of what goes on in the South in the sense that Highlander's been involved in the things of significance that happened in the South. When there's nothing happening, then Highlander was not doing any movement-type activities because there was no movement. We followed pretty closely what's happened to the people.

But if we only followed that, we would have no educational role. We've always tried to find little pockets of progressivism, little pockets of radicalism, something that was a little different than just survival. In so doing, when a situation started forming, Highlander was inside that movement, not waiting for it to happen and then trying to be a part of it. For example, during the civil rights period, through the Citizenship Schools, workshops, and the fact that Highlander was an inte-

grated place, many who became leaders of the civil
rights movement had been at Highlander, and Highlander was accepted as a part of it. We were not something outside asking what can we do to help or can we
get on the band wagon. It was just taken for granted
that activists could count on Highlander and make use
of Highlander. Same thing happened in the early days
of the industrial union movement.

So the valley periods can be used just to kill time
and survive, or they can be used to lay the groundwork
of being inside when a movement occurs. That's what
makes it possible for us to have peak periods. I remember so well so many people, educators, people of good
will during the civil rights period who rushed in after
the band wagon started and climbed up on top of the
band wagon and were part of the movement. But the
movement was being run by the people inside and they
couldn't get inside because people didn't know them inside, and they didn't have time then to get acquainted
and to build trust. It was too late. In a crisis situation,
you only deal with the people you can trust.

When you're trying to build for the future, that's the
creative period. I always have valued those low periods
when you had to really struggle intellectually to try to
get the sense of what was going on, so you could find
little pockets to work in. That's the only way you'll ever
be part of the struggle, when you climb the hill out of
the valley. So Highlander, seems to me, has been a part
of the people's lives whether they're in the valley or on
the hill. During the low periods—what I call the organizational periods, the individualistic periods, not the

movement periods—the people, not only us but every-body, are longing for something better. Trying to get a hold of something, trying to make something. Today I was glad you had those presentations of the activities that are being done here, because to my mind some of those activities may well have the seeds of moving from services and limited reforms to structural reforms. The reason I say some of them may have that seed is because there's enough anger in some of them; there's enough understanding that the system isn't ever going to serve their purpose; that they may develop into some pro-grams for structural changes, conscious of the fact that they're against the system and they're trying to change the system. Being in a valley period, an organizational period, doesn't mean Highlander has any less impor-tant role. It means it's a different role, a harder role. Highlander's history has been up and down but not important and unimportant. We would never have the importance, the recognition that we have gotten if we hadn't done these jobs in the valleys. It's always been an identification with the people. When the people are high, we are high, hopefully a little above them. When they're low, we're down low, but hopefully we're a little above them. Low periods are a good time to work out the techniques and ways of involving people, ways of having people begin to use critical judgments. In a movement period, it's too late after you get going to stop and do these things. People are too busy doing something else.

I'm much better at working out ideas in action than I am in theorizing about it and then transferring my thinking to action. I don't work that way. I work with tentative ideas and I experiment and then with that experimentation in action, I finally come to the conclusions about what I think is the right way to do it. This is an effort to express what I learned by the way I have of learning—that's in action, testing out ideas, seeing what works, seeing what doesn't. And, of course, all along there's always a theory for everything, before you act you know there's a connection. But those are little theories that finally build up to a bigger theory. I can say that theory didn't come out of my head. That came out of action. That came out of interaction, theory, practice, reflection, which you describe so well. That's the result and not the cause. And it's still subject to constant change. As action, I'm enlightened by the things I learn working with people in action.

"It's necessary to laugh with the people"

MYLES: Paulo, as I understood your question to me, it was in many ways, "How did you become Myles Horton?" Would you like to respond and talk about some of the ways that you became Paulo Freire and all the many ways that you've reinvented your life out of your experiences?

PAULO: You started by saying that it was not easy. I also say that it's not easy for me, but I can try to say something about that. As in your case, I also learned a lot from difficulties. In my childhood I had some problems concerning not eating enough, and my family suffered—not too much but suffered—from the Depression of

1929. As a child I had some problems understanding what I was studying at the primary school. All these things helped me. You are right when you say sometimes a situation like this provokes bad reactions, sometimes good reactions; sometimes they help, sometimes they don't help. In my case I feel that I was helped. It was very interesting for me to understand what it meant to be hungry. I say that we know what it means to be hungry when we don't have the possibility to eat, when we don't see how to solve the challenge of being hungry. For example, I don't know what it means to be hungry if I am hungry just because I am on a diet to get a beautiful shape. It does not mean that I know what it means to be hungry because I can eat. It's a question of wanting to eat. We know what it means to be hungry when we don't know how to solve the problem, and I had that. I had this experience, and it helped me a lot. When I was 12 years old, I lived out of Recife. I shared my days with boys belonging to my social class and also with working-class boys. In some way I had the experience of mediating them, as I had been born to a middle-class family. From the point of view of being hungry, I was next to the working-class boys, and I could understand well the two situations. Since that time, even though I could not understand the real reasons, I began to think that something was wrong. Maybe I can vocalize the beginnings of my commitment as an educator fighting against injustice. Maybe I can locate these beginnings in my childhood because it was there that I started learning that it was important to fight against this. I did not know yet how to fight as well as I do today—though I don't know too much today!—but I began to be open to this kind of learning when I was a child. I am sure of that.

There is another point, I think, that is important for me when I try to understand myself and my way of acting, of fighting. Side by side with the experience of my childhood, like in the case of Myles, is the experience of my parents. That is, how they loved themselves and how they gave us, the sons, the example of loving, and how they loved us. When I remember my childhood, in spite of the difficulties we had to eat well, to dress well, to study; I felt emotionally entire. I had emotional equilibrium, and I am sure that it was due to the relationships of my parents with us and between themselves. I am totally convinced about that. The more we get this kind of alive love among parents, the more it's possible to help kids to grow up in good shape. Of course, this kind of love has to be built. I don't believe in love as a mere gift. That is, I had to love really Elza, and Elza had to love really me, and we had to learn how to love ourselves.

MYLES: You had to work at it.

PAULO: We had to work on that. When we got married in 1944, I remember the time we spent learning how to go beyond the conflicts without denying them. That is, how to learn from the conflicts, how to learn to become ourselves in a different way. The question for those who love themselves is not to collapse one into the other. It's not the question. The question is how to continue to be myself and for Elza to be herself, differently each one but at the same time being something that belonged to us. In other words, it was possible for us to be artists and creators of a common existence with respect for the individuality and preferences of each person. I could not impose on Elza my preference, my style, my way of expressing my feelings. I was much more open than Elza. Elza felt strongly about every thing, but it was easier for me to express my feelings. I had to respect her and she had to respect me. Do you see? It was a beautiful experience. I am sure that we have to learn together, patiently, with humility, how to build our common existence, because when we get married we have to create a new world. It's no longer my world. It's no longer her world. It is our world now that must be created, and our world will become the world of the kids who come into life because of our responsibility. Magdalena was born 41 years ago because of a great love between me and Elza. I learned when I was a child that a loving space is indispensable for development of the children. When I got married to Elza, I already knew about that, but I had to confirm with Elza that we would raise our children this way. We fought a lot, not against ourselves, but to create this kind of comprehension, in order for the children to be themselves.

All these things are together, but methodologically I am making them separate. The second influence, as I said, was the harmony and the contradictions between my father and my mother. Both of them were people from the last century, and they were absolutely open in the first part of the century. I was born in 1921, and the way they educated us was an anticipation from the pedagogical point of view. They were beyond the much more rigid patterns of living with kids. I had a very warm and open atmosphere, which helped me. This is the second element that helped me understand myself, and look, I am giving emphasis to these elements and not to some intellectual elements, which are also very important for me.

The third element inside of this atmosphere was the religious background, the Christian background. Thinking about this element of my formation, I think that it's interesting to underline two aspects. One is the consistency that my parents demanded between proclaiming faith and having consistent behavior vis-à-vis this faith. Because of this, I began also to demand consistency. I remember that when I was 6 years old, one day I was talking with my father and my mother, and I protested strongly against the way my grandmother had treated a black woman at home—not with physical violence, but with undoubtedly racial prejudice. I said to my mother and to my father that I couldn't understand that, not maybe with the formal speech I am using now, but I was underlining for me the impossibility of being a Christian and at the same time discriminating against another person for any reason. I was very angry. I remember that my mother used to say to me, after the death of my father, that my father always said to her, "This boy will become a subversive." He didn't say revolutionary. He used to say subversive. I liked it.

MYLES: That was real insight.

PAULO: Yes. And there is another point concerning religion

243

that I have emphasized sometimes in some writings, which was the tolerance of my father. Consistency and tolerance as virtues. Why do I speak about tolerance? I began to learn the meaning of this revolutionary virtue from him when I was a child. Why? Because my mother had a Catholic upbringing, and he was a spiritualist from France. He had another understanding of Christ. He did not choose to go to church. He had nothing to do with the church, Catholic or Protestant. My mother had a broad vision of the world. Philosophically, he had another compassion, but he respected her totally. It's very important, because as I told you they came from last century in a very male-dominated culture in which the choices of men had to be imposed on the women. Still today it is like this. Of course the young generation in Brazil fortunately is fighting against that. He never imposed his beliefs on my mother and on us, but we discussed both of their ideas. This is very important to underline, because sometimes the person who imposes can have a kind of irresponsible behavior or attitude, and for me it's very bad. In some instances, maybe not imposing is worse than imposing, because if you impose you can create reaction, but if you don't impose and you do nothing, maybe you don't create any kind of re-action. It's very bad from the point of view of *formation*. In my father's case, no. He did not impose on us, but he discussed with us his positions and then my mother's positions, for example. When I remember how I grew up in this atmosphere of respect, a presence which re-spected the other presence, I see it was important for my development as an educator. It was not difficult for me to understand that as an educator I should respect the students, because I had been respected by my father and my mother. It was not difficult, for example, to know that in trying to teach adults to read and to write, I should start from their words, because my father and my mother taught me in the backyard of the house from my words and not from their words. All these things helped me a lot to theorize many of the things that I lived—something that I would have to do later, and I am still engaged in this process.

When I went first to meet with workers and peasants in Recife's slums, to teach them and to learn from them, I have to confess that I did that pushed by my Christian faith. I feel there are people who speak about Christ with such a facility. There are people who say, "Yesterday I met Christ on the corner." Oh, I don't meet Christ every day. Only unless Christ is in lots of miserable people, exploited, dominated people. But Christ personally, himself, it's not so easy. I have some respect for that, but I have to say that I went first as if I had been sent. Look, I know that I had been sent, but Christ did not do that personally with me. I don't want to say that I have such prestige. I went because I believed in what I heard and in what I studied. I could not be still. I thought that I should do something, and what happened is that the more I went to the slum areas, the more I talked with the people, the more I learned from the people. I got the conviction that the people were sending me to Marx. The people never did say, "Paulo, please why do you not go to read Marx?" No. The people never said that, but their reality said that to me. The misery of the reality. The tremendous domination, the exploitation. Even the very magical religious position of the people, understanding misery to be a kind of test that God was imposing in order to know whether they continued to be good sons—even this sent me to Marx. That is, I had to come running into Marx. Then I began to read Marx and to read about Marx, and the more I did that the more I became convinced that we really would have to change the structures of reality, that we should become absolutely committed to a global process of transformation. But what is interesting in my case—this is not the case of all the people whose background is similar to mine—my "meetings" with Marx never suggested to me to stop "meeting" Christ. I never said to Marx: "Look, Marx, really Christ was a baby. Christ was naive." And also I never said to Christ, "Look, Marx was a materialistic and terrible man." I always spoke to both of them in a very loving way. You see, I feel comfortable in this position. Sometimes people say to me that I am contradictory. My answer is that I have the right to be contradictory, and secondly, I don't consider myself contradictory in this. No, I'm absolutely clear. It was very important for me, and it has been and continues to be. If you ask me, then, if I am a religious man, I say no, I'm not a religious man. They understand religious as religion-like. I would say that I am a man of faith. I take care with this. I feel myself very comfortable with this.

Of course, I had my academic experiences. I had my readings and I continued to have my readings. I learned a lot from Marx, but I never accepted being taught by Marx without asking serious questions also. Critical thinking is required. Thinking cannot be closed, put inside of something. It cannot be immobilized; to do so would be tremendously contradictory to what I think and do.

And finally, to finish this confession, I would say that, like Myles, the greatest source for all the things together helping me really is and was the relationships with the people.

MYLES: Love of people.

PAULO: Loving people. It's very dialectical. The first sources I spoke about were important for me, but in going to the slums and to the peasants I had to be consistent with the reasons why I went there. I did not have any other door but to love the people—that is, loving people, believing in the people, but not in a naive way. To be able to accept that all these things the people do are good just because people are people? No, the people also commit mistakes. I don't know many things, but it's necessary to believe in the people. It's necessary to laugh with the people because if we don't do that, we cannot learn from the people, and in not learning from the people we cannot teach them. This is why I feel so linked to this experience, this work here in Highlander, and also why I feel so comfortable talking with Myles. In the last analysis, I think that we are relatives, we are sons of the same source.

MYLES: Yes that's right.

PAULO: With difference that makes us better!

MYLES: I'm going to read a short little poem here. You can figure out who wrote it. "Go to the people. Learn from them. Live with them. Love them. Start with what they know. Build with what they have. But the best of leaders when the job is done, when the task is accomplished, the people will all say we have done it ourselves." Who wrote that? Who could have written it?

THIRD PARTY: You could have written it. Paulo could have written it.

MYLES: It's taken a long time for people to come to these ideas hasn't it? This was written in 604 B.C. by Lao Tzu. Isn't it wonderful? That's a translation, of course, but the ideas are exactly what Paulo and I've been talking about. That's wonderful.

Epilogue

MYLES: Well, you feel contented that we've done all we can do?

PAULO: Oh yes. Maybe I'm totally wrong, but I think that it will be a beautiful book.

MYLES: Yes. I don't see any reason for having any more discussions.

PAULO: It is more or less structured.

MYLES: Let's have a drink.

PAULO: Yes.

Index

Index

Horton, Myles (*cont.*)
enced by readings, 34–36;
McCarthy era, xvi, xxviii,
205; Ozone, 48–51; parent-
ing, xviii–xix, 139–141;
parents of, 13; religious influences, 28, 33; vision and
strategy, 196–197
Horton, Thorsten, 139–141,
183, 191–192
Horton, Zilphia (Zilphia Mae
Johnson), xx, 41n, 140,
166, 192
Humanity: of charismatic
leaders, 111; meaning
of, 100

Ideas: acceptance by the
people, 107; exposure to,
107; imposing on others,
105, 106–107
Illiteracy: as justification for
racial discrimination (U.S.),
84; as justification for
social-class discrimination
(Brazil), 84

Jenkins, Esau, xxiv, 67–76,
82, 91. *See also* Citizenship
Schools
Justus, May, 183–184

King, Martin Luther, xxiv, xxviii, 75, 114; as charismatic
leader, 109, 112
Knowledge (knowing): from
books and conversation,
99; as dialectical, 101; discovering the need for, 66;
as historical, 193–194; importance of, 57; need for
practice, 98; of the people,
65, 98, 150; use and sharing
of, 235. *See also* Education;
Educator

Labor movement, 110, 114,
123; in Brazil, xxv–xxvi;
industrial union move-
ment, 110; involvement
with Highlander, 163–
169; labor education, xxiv,
34; workers' education in
Brazil, 63, 65
Lao Tzu, 248
Leadership: characteristics of,
185; role of, 181–182
Learning: from each other,
49, 55; from experience
and reading, 40–41; im-
portance of atmosphere,
92–93; from the people,
46–47; process of, 40–41;
resulting from mobilizing
and organizing, 117
Lewis, Helen, 179
Lindeman, Eduard, 53; *The
Meaning of Adult Educa-
tion*, 53n
Literacy: group vs. individualistic approach, 91–92; as
means of personal identity,
90; national literacy cam-
paigns, 93–94; National
Literacy Program (Plan),
xxii, xxvii; political aspects,
91; popular education, xxii
Lynd, Robert, 10–11

Machado, Antonio, 6n
Malcolm X, as charismatic
leader, 109–112
Marx, Karl, 191; as influence
on Freire, 245–246; Marx-
ism as means to analyze
society, 35–36, 102, 232.
See also Horton, Myles
Memmi, Albert, *The Colonizer
and the Colonized*, 36
Merrifield, Juliet, 170
Mobilizing, 110; as differing
from organizing, 117; as

educational process, 117–118; used to learn from the people, 122

Morris, Aldon, *The Origins of the Civil Rights Movement*, xxv

National Labor Relations Board, 165

Neutrality: as immoral act, 102–105; people or institutions claiming to be neutral, 133, 185–186; pertaining to education, 64, 104, 180; pertaining to knowing, 23. *See also* Ideas

Nicaragua, 208, 216–226; popular education programs, 13, 223–225; revolution, 77, 216–217

Niebuhr, Reinhold, xx, xxiii, 42; *Moral Man in Immoral Society*, 103

Nyerere, Julius, 219

Occupational health movement, 128

Oldendorf, Sandra Brenneman, 89n

Organizations: for changing the system, 185; as first step toward social movement, 124

Organizing: characteristics of organizer, 124–126; differing from education, 115, 119, 127; differing from mobilizing, 117; as educational process, 117–119, 121; used to disempower, 120

Ozone (Tenn.), 48–51, 55. *See also* Horton, Myles

Parks, Rosa, xxiv, 153

Participatory research: as

education, 120; in organizing, 122

Phenix, Lucy Massie, *You Got to Move*, 170n

Power: of adult society, 184; in choosing educational program, 107–109; and co-optation, 206; of the group, 166–167; and participation of the masses, 97; in process of mobilizing, 110; and science, 105

Presbyterian Sunday School Board, 47

Reading, 30–37; books as theoretical instruments, 31; as research, 37; of a text, 37, 158; of text vs. content, 31–32

Recife (Brazil), xv, xvii, xxvi, 25–26, 65, 67, 150, 209, 240, 245; literacy program, 77–78, 82–84, 87–89, 92–93; workers' education, 65. *See also* Freire, Paulo

Recife, University of, xx, xxii

Religion: influences, xx, 243–246; interaction with social action, 243

Respect: as basis of Citizenship Schools, 69–70; for knowledge of the people, 101; for people, 66; for students, 61

Robinson, Bernice, 71–76, 78–82, 85–86, 89–91, 156. *See also* Citizenship Schools

Romasco, Ann, 79

Savannah (Tenn.), 12, 18, 20

Science: and power, 105; social dimension of, 105; virtues of beauty and simplicity, 32

Shelley, *Prometheus Unbound*, 34–35. *See also* Horton, Myles

Social change: radical challenge for action, 94; radical transformation of society as a process, 216; relationship to learning, 102; transition from old to new society, 218; use of time, 222
Social equality, 134
South (U.S.), xvii–xxiv, 44, 67, 134, 153–154, 231, 236
Southern Christian Leadership Conference, role in Citizenship Schools, xxv, xxix, 75–76. *See also* Citizenship Schools
Student Non-Violent Coordinating Committee, 113

Teaching, 160; clarifying role of teacher, 104, 142; and discovery, 193; contents of, in historical and social context, 108; vs. education, 62–63; fundamental role of teacher, 23; as inseparable from educating, 188; knowing the issues being taught, 59; "political clarity," 91; relationship between teaching, giving knowledge, and learning knowledge, 151; in

social context, 104–105. *See also* Education; Educator; Knowledge
Theory: as dialectical, 101; importance of, 100; resulting from action and reflection, 239
Thinking: critically, 172–174; and decision making, 164; outside conventional frameworks, 44–45
Thompson, John, 41
Thrasher, Sue, 91
Tjerandsen, Carl, *Education for Citizenship: A Foundation's Experience*, 82n

UNESCO, evaluating adult literacy, 77
Union Theological Seminary, xx, 42

Vygotsky, Lev, *Thought and Language*, 36

West, Don, xxii
Witnesses for Peace, 223–224

Young, Andrew, 75–76, 113. *See also* Citizenship Schools